getting older better

getting
older
better

The Best
Advice
Ever on
Money,
Health,
Creativity,
Sex,
Work,
Retirement,
and More

PAMELA D. BLAIR, PHD

HAMPTON ROADS

Copyright © 2005, 2014 by Pamela D. Blair.

Cover design: www.levanfisherdesign.com/Barbara Fisher
Cover art © shutterstock/paul_june
Interior designed by Deborah Dutton

Hampton Roads Publishing Company, Inc.
Charlottesville, VA 22906
Distributed by Red Wheel/Weiser, LLC
www.redwheelweiser.com

Sign up for our newsletter and special offers by going to
www.redwheelweiser.com/newsletter/.

ISBN: 978-1-57174-703-7
Library of Congress Cataloging-in-Publication Data available upon request.

Printed on acid-free paper in the United States of America.
EBM

10 9 8 7 6 5 4 3 2 1

This book is dedicated to my Swedish grandmother, Agda Matilda Janssen Smith, and to my four sisters, Marilyn, Susie, Debbie, and Alison.

contents

introduction

I have always longed to be old, and that is because all my life I have had such great exemplars of old age, such marvelous models to contemplate.

—MAY SARTON

I remember my Swedish grandmother's strength and steadfastness. A pioneer in a new world, she had to be tough. As a nineteen-year-old immigrant, she came to the United States in the early 1900s on her own. She married and later became a widow with a five-year-old daughter to care for. As I faced some of my own life challenges (two divorces, a husband who died, raising children on my own), I drew strength from her story. As she aged, I watched her seek ways to grow intellectually (she loved US history, listening to books on tape when she could no longer see well enough to read) and socially (in her seventies, she had a boyfriend who was in his sixties!). She walked everywhere and dressed with class. She enjoyed politics, creative pursuits, saving money to buy quality items, teaching, and playing with her grandchildren. She died at 102. I'm grateful to her for giving me a solid, healthy view of aging.

My sister Marilyn has also given me glimpses into what I might expect as I age. As mentor and pathfinder for me, she's been like an efficient snowplow, clearing and sanding the road ahead of me for safe travel. As grateful as I am to her, the five-year glimpse ahead that she offered hasn't felt like quite enough. I've wanted to know more. I've wanted to know more about what was waiting for me in the years ahead so I could plan, aspire to greater things, feel some measure of control, and be part of an evolving community of women. May Sarton called them "great exemplars of old age" and had them all her life. I realized after entering the second half of my life that other than Grandma and Marilyn, I lacked "marvelous models to contemplate."

This book was born out of a search for more role models. I wondered, *What will old age and its unknown future with its specter of diminishments of all kinds demand of me? Where is the dignity to be found in it? What can I expect at various stages? How will I approach death—my own and that of those I love? What passions do I have time to pursue?*

Women over fifty are the new pioneers. Author Colette Dowling says, "Because no previous generation of midlife women had the luxury of seeing decades of productive time roll out before them, we who came of age with the women's movement are in the position, once again, of having to do it for the first time." We are living longer and better lives than ever before. As there is no turning back the clock, the goal is to live these golden years the best we can, maintaining our quality of life and independence for as long as possible.

Medical advances coupled with technological research are going to extend our life expectancies so much that some of us could easily reach 120. We might become the first generation of women to live sixty or so years beyond menopause! The length of time that humans spend in adulthood has more than doubled since the early part of the 20th century, making it possible for today's midlife women to have fifty more years with their mates (or without them), of watching their children grow old, and of facing career choices, leisure time, physical challenges, and learning opportunities—and fifty more years of trying to fund it all.

In the next fifty years, as science, medicine, and bioengineering extend the span of human life, one-hundredth birthdays will lose their mystique. In 1950, there were only 2,300 people older than one hundred. By 2050, there could be somewhere in the neighborhood of 600,000 centenarians in the United States. By mid-century, old people will outnumber young people for the first time in history. The 20th century has given us the gift of longevity. In the past hundred years, life expectancy has increased by three decades, a phenomenon that is reshaping our families, attitudes, work lives, and institutions.

We live in a paradoxical time. In the past, respect for the wisdom of the elders was central to human societies. The elders served as keepers of cultural knowledge. But today, in technological countries such as ours, respect has faded into bare tolerance as we expect older people to act, look, and talk young. This view is changing slowly, and aging, as we have known it, will no longer only be seen as a time of disability, mental decline, and diminished energy.

We will be living longer—much, much longer—than we ever dreamed possible. This new era of aging will create an altogether new set of challenges. Our families and social institutions will be boggled by a social revolution. About every seven seconds, a baby boomer turns sixty. Retirement is becoming passé, just another word for "career change," eighty-year-olds are dating and marrying, and ninety-year-olds are getting college degrees. Thanks to the miracles of medical science, we are experiencing an extension of the human life span, and people age one hundred or older are surprisingly healthy. We are beginning to see more and more educated and healthy older people in our society.

Before the 19th century, most people didn't age much—they died. Just a hundred years ago, few reached age sixty-five. Now there are about 35 million Americans who are sixty-five and older. By 2030, more than 70 million Americans will be over the age of sixty-five. The number of people over sixty-five has grown tenfold since 1900. And the fastest growing segment of our population is the eighty-five-and-over age group.

Aging continues to be redefined, and we need new words to describe it. In writing this book, I've struggled to find a single word for age fifty-plus women that isn't negative. Authorities on aging describe us as being young until we're forty, middle-aged between forty and sixty, and old from sixty to eighty. But those terms are simultaneously broad and limiting. We need better words that embody the spirit of the woman over fifty. Some suggest using the word *crone,* but many women bristle at that.

I find the term *wise woman* appealing. Helen Hayes, first lady of the American theater, who died in 1993 at the age of ninety-three, thought we should be called maturians. For her, the word implied there was "still a bit of fight in us." Marilyn, my sister, doesn't like the words *old* or *older;* I like the word *elder.* Some Native Americans use the term *Grandmother Moon,* the elderwoman of the tribe. Perhaps we could settle on the term *elderwoman.* Instead of the clinical designation of *postmenopausal,* we might use the term *opal* (Older People with an Active Lifestyle), coined by Frances Lear, publisher of *Lear's Magazine.* I like the idea of being opalescent—a gem emitting fire! I also like the idea of changing the word *aging* to *evolving,* or as my eighty-year-old friend Alma says, "ripening."

If the world turns in your favor, you could potentially live out all the hidden aspects of your personality, explore your passions, pursue your yearnings to see the planet or change the world, express your unused talents, serve others, continue your search for love and knowledge—lots of possibilities lie in wait.

In preparing this book, I spoke with older women from all walks of life: professionals, homemakers, retirees, grandmothers, widows, single women. The issues I've written about are common to many of us. The women I interviewed said a book like this is needed. I am thankful to those women. I've come to realize that my aging experiences are not as unique as I had imagined and that I am not alone in my journey.

I had my grandmother and Marilyn to look to, yet I wanted more. I searched for other stories, experiences, and advice written by older women that could inform and inspire me. The majority of books written for women on aging have contained quotes and literary images from the writings of men. But a woman's experience of aging is different from a man's, so in the pages that follow, you will find heartfelt excerpts, quotes, stories, fun ideas, and serious philosophies written only by women—women authors and poets and wonderful folks of all kinds who will enrich and inform your aging experience. I hope the results of my personal search will enhance your life and that you will be inspired in your eldering and your evolving.

We are pioneers of a new age, and we are the foremothers of millions of women. For the sake of our daughters and generations of women still unborn, we have an assignment to make clear our role in society: to inscribe the possibilities of age on the guideposts to the future. What we create in our mature lives will be our gift to them. Join me in blazing a trail, in creating a legacy of wisdom and strength that can be passed on to the next generation of pioneer women in a new world.

how to use this book

Getting Older Better contains short essays on a broad range of topics that relate specifically to women and aging. Some deal with serious issues; others are meant to be entertaining and lighthearted. You may laugh, you may cry, but most importantly you will realize that you are not alone.

Depending on where you are in your personal journey, some topics may not be relevant to you. Some may be difficult to approach, as you are encouraged to look at issues often ignored. Read the ones that relate to you at this time in your life, and skip the ones that do not apply to you now. For instance, you may not be a grandmother (or a mother), so you might want to skip the essays on those topics.

Each essay is followed by questions that encourage you to journal your reactions, feelings, or what actions you might need to take. You are encouraged to respond to the questions honestly. Allow time for reflection on each topic and time to thoughtfully contemplate your responses. Studies suggest that journal writing, which focuses on deep thoughts and feelings about life events, can even reduce arthritic symptoms and increase immune function, and writing out thoughts and feelings can significantly improve the health of those with chronic illness.

This book is designed to take you through a process of understanding yourself in relation to aging. I present the more hopeful, exciting, and interesting aspects of aging alongside the more difficult ones. *Getting Older Better* is intended to be used along with a personal journal. However, you might think of your journal as a written legacy that, when completed, can be handed down to your daughters or to any younger woman with whom you have a relationship. As you write out your thoughts and answers, you will gain creative, practical ideas for your future. You will gain deeper insight into how you might, with personal integrity, structure the next years of your life.

part I

1
thoughts, cultural attitudes, and myths about women aging

One can *remain alive long past the usual date of disintegration if one is unafraid of change, insatiable in intellectual curiosity, interested in big things, and happy in small ways.*

—Edith Wharton

Many people who embrace living still hold on to negative impressions or myths about aging. Living passionately and well doesn't stop at a certain point in one's life, to be followed only by the destructive forces of aging. The sooner we change our attitude about this, the sooner we can honestly explore our longevity.

The attitude that surrounds us is that old age in its most problematic sense starts somewhere between fifty and sixty. Why is this? Perhaps we still buy into the outdated rule that midlife is the beginning of our decline. This fallacy is based on the equally outdated life expectancy of forty-seven years or so, which was an average life span at the beginning of the 20th century. Although average life expectancy has increased drastically since then, our cultural attitudes have not.

People who think positively about aging tend to live almost eight years longer than those who think negatively. In fact, thinking positively is a more significant life extender than low blood pressure, low cholesterol, exercising regularly, or not smoking. Feistiness also makes aging easier, and personal determination to stay independent can help overcome physical frailty. A study I read found that an optimistic attitude has a measurable effect on preventing heart disease, for instance.

We may not have control over a lot of things as we age, but what we do have control over is our *attitude* toward aging. The degenerative aspects of the aging process can be substantially retarded by a combination of factors that include improving attitude, taking opportunities for service, continuing intellectual stimulation, and adopting good health habits. Let's get started.

WHEN THEY WERE OUR AGE

We're suffering from an image of aging that comes from a different time. An image that was never anything but propaganda.

—Barbara Sher

We won't be experiencing aging the way our mothers and grandmothers did. Once again, we are defining our times. With some effort, we can be fit, fabulous, and over fifty. Our perception (and experience) of aging has changed because just about nothing in our lives is what it would have been in the lives of women our age even twenty years ago. For the most part, women now are healthier as they expect to live longer, reevaluate their priorities, and once again explore their passions.

Actress Susan Sarandon once said: "It's thrilling to know that around the world, women everywhere are working, thinking, daring, creating, making change. I don't know if our mothers ever felt this way about their counterparts—but I have the feeling our daughters will." We live in a wondrous age. Most women who reach age one hundred do so in surprisingly robust health. Genes may be responsible for about 30 percent of the physiological changes that occur in advanced age, but the majority of changes are the result of environment, diet, exercise, utilization of available medical care, and mental outlook.

My grandmother and my mother were my models of aging women. It was inconceivable to me that I would ever be as old as they seemed to be. I realize that I'm now the same age as my grandmother was back then, but it feels very different for me than I think it was for her. As I age, I intend to be more aware of my mental, emotional, and physical needs than my mother was of hers. I won't ignore my health as she did; I'll eat better, exercise to keep up my strength and balance, and not allow anyone to take advantage of me. She smoked heavily, was constantly stressed, and died at seventy-eight. I hope to live many years longer than she did.

How is your experience of aging different than your mother's or grandmother's?

MYTHS TO NOT LIVE BY

The media reflects our collective anxiety about growing older. I like to call this the "misery myth."

—Laura L. Carstensen, PhD

To age successfully, we need to be aware of the newer and older myths about aging that our current culture holds true. Here are some examples of the myths I've heard and what I know to be true:

Myth: Old women are depressed and lonely.

Truth: Depending on circumstances, we may get sad and lonely from time to time, but the research shows that the least lonely and depressed women are over seventy-five.

Myth: Older women are less successful in new pursuits.

Truth: Some of the best and brightest women, though past the half-century mark in years, are still climbing the ladder of success in the world.

Myth: Old women have more stress in their lives.

Truth: According to psychologists, older women have more stress-free days than younger women do.

Myth: Growing older is synonymous with the loss of meaning and purpose.

Truth: Research and the elderly themselves are demonstrating that a person's later years can be the richest ever in wisdom and spirituality.

Myth: If you are older and are reminiscing or becoming garrulous about the past, you are exhibiting signs of senility.

Truth: These recollections are natural and appropriate. Their purpose is to resolve life conflicts and to do a life review.

Myth: The older you get, the faster time passes.

Truth: Mathematically, those proverbial endless summers of your childhood were not even one minute longer than last summer. You have more routines now, and routines lend uniformity, which makes it very easy to be oblivious to time.

Myth: Everyone wants to, and should be willing to, hear our wisdom and opinions just because we are older.

Truth: Even though we're older and wiser, we don't necessarily know everything.

Myth: Older women are weak and have to be protected.

Truth: Once the protector myth is conquered, women become whole and authentic. We know that if we accept a limiting role, we violate ourselves.

Myth: Creativity is only for the gifted few, and our talents dim with age.

Truth: Creativity is not just for geniuses and the gifted. It is the energy that allows us to express ourselves in unique ways; it enables us to view life as an opportunity for exploration, and it knows no age.

Myth: All old women are physically passionless and have no interest in being sexual.

Truth: Many older women continue to be passionate about life and maintain an interest in sex.

Think about another myth you have heard about women and aging. Then write about what you've learned is true.

LIVING IN THE PRESENT

You can't know who you are if you don't spend time honoring yourself, and living in the present.

—Naomi Judd

Do you think about some event that might happen in the future that causes you to feel anxious and uncomfortable? Doesn't that kind of fretting keep you from enjoying what's available in the present? Sure, we have to make plans for our financial and health care needs and things of that nature. But once the plans are in place, it's important to be mindful of how you torture yourself out of the present and the beauty it brings.

I wonder how I will be as a very old woman, and some of what I envision worries me. I wonder how I'll manage if I'm infirm or unable to walk or see well. In those moments, I work at bringing myself back to the present, which is all we are assured of anyway. I keep reminding myself that every moment stands alone, a presence in its own right, a singular visitation that doesn't include the future.

We're getting older every day, but we need something else to think about besides long-term-care insurance and wondering what our adult kids are doing when we're home alone. Sue Bender wrote in *Everyday Sacred: A Woman's Journey Home*, "The challenge is to find even ten minutes when the world stops, and for that moment, there is nothing else. How can we bring that quality to what time we have—making that limited time sacred?"

Take a moment—right now. Perhaps you're reading this book in a chair, on a train, or in a plane. Are you comfortable? Does the chair feel soft or hard? What do you see around you? Are you in a beautiful location? On a beach or a porch? Pay close attention to the small, the beautiful, the meaningful. Live in the present—for today, for ten minutes, for an hour.

What have you been overlooking in the present because you've been too worried about the future?

CHANGING TEMPO

I used to be able, as most women are, to do four or five things at once. Do the juggling act. Now, if I can keep one plate in the air, that's good.

—Ursula K. Le Guin

A respected colleague, seventy-nine-year-old Anne, told me she wonders why she's tired. As an alcohol abuse counselor, she sees four or five clients a day, attends training lectures or presents at them, keeps her own home, and volunteers at a women's shelter. She's tired and hasn't learned the fine art of pacing herself, of dancing to a slower (no-less productive) tempo.

Each week we have 168 hours—10,080 minutes—to work and play, and you spend the better part of your time trying to get too much done—rushing, dashing, scurrying. In the mid-20th century, futurists predicted that computers and other labor-saving devices would free up time and transform America into the most leisurely society in history. Exactly the opposite happened.

In this age of rapidly expanding technology and continued consumerism, how can you fashion a simpler, slower-paced life? If you buzz from this chore to that with cell phone in hand, racing from one activity to the next, how can you enjoy your world?

I look for opportunities each day to see the world a little more clearly. This is my private time to enjoy the quietness of just being, of stopping to look and to feel and to think—and to indulge myself in a changing tempo.

The societal expectation that we must be accomplishing something all the time is broadcast so efficiently and from such an early age that we internalize it. We struggle with a seditious inner voice that says, "You're wasting time. Get up and do something with your life."

We're expected (or we expect ourselves) to respond to a fast-paced life in the same way we did when were twenty. Are we obliged to keep up with the latest in technological advances such as texting, Twittering, and Facebooking so as not to be out of step? Or do we have the privilege by virtue of age of opting out or being selective in our adoption of this new wave of fast-paced technology?

Try slowing the tempo down once in a while. Personally, I prefer pen and paper for personal letters even though communicating by email is faster and more convenient. I like holding a real book in my hands instead of an electronic reading device. I enjoy meandering slowly through a gift shop, touching and smelling the trinkets, and smiling at the cashier. Yet, I also enjoy ordering online and not having to fight the crowds during the holidays!

It feels essential to my well-being at this time in my life to slow the tempo a bit. My children are completely launched, my writing and counseling career are going well, and I feel fortunate to not have to care for older parents, so I have time to indulge myself. I must admit, I like the new pace.

How do you feel about changing tempo?

BEING VULNERABLE

Pay attention to your gut feelings—the gut doesn't lie. And, by all means, don't be afraid to say "no"!

—MARILYN HOUSTON

Each year, thousands of Americans over fifty fall prey to a wide variety of scams. The most common type of frauds committed against older Americans are email phishing, telemarketing, and mailbox scams (i.e., illegal sweepstakes, bogus charities, unlicensed health insurers, investment scams, and deceptive lotteries). Here are some recent examples quoted from *www.snopes.com* (a great website to check out if you're unsure about the validity of an offer):

- Nigerian Scam: A wealthy foreigner who needs help moving millions of dollars from his homeland promises a hefty percentage of this fortune as a reward for assisting him.

- Foreign Lottery Scam: Announcements inform recipients that they've won large sums of money in foreign lotteries.

- Secret Shopper Scam: Advertisers seek applicants for paid positions as "secret" or "mystery" shoppers.

- Work-at-Home Scam: Advertisers offer kits that enable home workers to make money posting links on the Internet.

- Family Member in Distress Scam: Scammers impersonate distressed family members in desperate need of money.

Older women are sometimes considered easy targets for con artists because we don't want to be considered rude—we were taught to be nice at all costs. Some are at a disadvantage because they live alone or are desperate for money to meet some need.

For example, we often lack the skills to end a phone call when we feel pressure from the person on the other end of the line. Are you sometimes reluctant to hang up the phone or say, "No, thank you," because you're afraid of offending someone? I have no problem deleting email, reporting spam, and hanging up the phone. It took practice, but now the older I get, the easier it gets!

Not all business and investment seminars are scams. One of the key warning signs is being told you'll get rich quickly, that you'll earn up to $100,000 a year, that no experience or training is necessary, that the program will deliver security for years to come, or that it worked for hundreds of others, including the seminar leaders.

The Federal Trade Commission is working hard to prevent us from becoming victims of these schemes. Local agencies have stepped up their efforts to combat the problem, and several states have laws that make scams against senior citizens a serious offense. But no commission or agency is a substitute for your own intuitive sense and willingness to say no.

What will you do if you sense that an offer of any kind isn't on the up-and-up?

AGING CAN BE FUN?

It really IS funny to see an adult looking all around the room for her glasses without noticing that they are on top of her head.

—HELEN HEIGHTSMAN GORDON

Is it possible that growing older can be fun? Perhaps our negative expectations have something to do with our experiences. Since my friend Joan turned fifty-five, she laments the aging process every chance she gets. She defines it solely as the breakdown of the body and its functions. She seems to be creating more discomfort for herself all the time—more aches, more pains, more visits to the doctor.

On the other hand, my over-eighty friend Tita talks of what is exciting, fulfilling, and fun in her life. When she has aches, she doesn't focus on them. She travels, she reads, she laughs, and she nurtures her relationships with her friends, children, and grandchildren.

I'm looking forward to becoming more outrageous, aches and pains and all. If I someday need to walk with a cane, it won't be an ordinary one. I'll paint it red and white to look like a candy cane. If I must use a walker, it will be equipped with a bicycle horn. Beep, beep—out of my way! If the arthritis in my hands bothers me, I'll wear green polka-dotted mittens indoors in the winter. Aging can be an outrageously validating experience if you learn to laugh at yourself and focus on the fun instead.

Write about something outrageous you could do to make aging more fun.

ACCEPTING CHANGE

Life is change. It will change around you if you don't change with it.

—Helen Gurley Brown

Everything is in a constant state of change—our bodies, homes, families, spiritual connections, and whole world. We can use our energies to fight and resist change. But there is something bold and strong about surrender. Change is inevitable, and resisting it causes our souls great sorrow and pain. While we're so busy resisting, we risk missing out on the potential for enormous joy.

There probably isn't a day that you're not acutely aware of change. Your body is changing, your family and friends are changing, your strength and speed of mental processing are changing, and your priorities are changing. How are you dealing with these changes? Denial? Acceptance?

As for me, if acceptance means approval, I say no, I don't approve of some of what is happening as I age. If acceptance means I will work change into my life, then I say yes. If change means painful loss and disappointment, I say no, I don't want any of that! (And do I have a choice?) If change means growth, forward movement, and a refreshed attitude, I say yes. If acceptance means I will let myself go as I age, then I say no.

Author Frances Weaver tells us it's our attitude toward all these changes that's most important. She wrote, "The sincere desire to lead a productive, interesting life at any age depends upon our own imagination and acceptance of new ideas."

If you embrace this time of dynamic change, you will feel more peaceful. You're on an adventure. Say yes to feeling peaceful—and say yes to adventure.

Write about how your life is changing.

AGE GRIEF

You know what surprises me most as I cycle through the fives stages of age grief? How did I . . . end up sounding like my parents?

—J. Eva Nagel

Shock, denial, anger, bargaining, and acceptance—these are the identified stages of grief. I find I am reluctant to believe the grief associated with aging is similar in its stages to the grief one feels around death, though. Yet after considering this a while, I believe it is.

One day I woke up to find that I was showing the inevitable signs of moving toward an older age. That's shock. Denial set in as I tried to stay up as late as I used to and when I tried to work all day in the garden without a rest. Certainly I had always been able to push myself when it came to physical work, but now I had to enjoy the same activities in shorter blocks of time. My denial didn't last long because I was too busy being angry. Angry that it was different now. Angry that my back and legs hurt after stooping over the weed patch. Angry that I was now falling asleep before ten p.m.!

Bargaining? Not sure about that one. I still haven't tried to bargain with my higher power to make me young again. I haven't said, "God, if you give me the energy and looks of a thirty-year-old, I'll pledge more money to charity." So, I'm working on acceptance. You see, I had planned on aging naturally, with grace and faith, with a nonattachment of sorts. I knew reincarnation and heaven were possibilities, so I wasn't so concerned with death. I don't take myself too seriously. My eyes are focused and wide open, yet some days I still mourn aspects of my younger years.

It's normal to miss our youth to some degree. Identify where you are in the process, and then give yourself permission to move through the grief and come out the other side energized and ready to face the future.

Are you grieving for your lost youth? What stage of age grief are you experiencing? What can you do to move through it?

AGES AND STAGES

There's something so liberating about this stage of life. It's not that you know more, necessarily; it's that you accept not knowing and experience a different kind of ease.

—SUSAN SARANDON

People are staying healthy and living longer, and the old stages of life no longer hold. According to some scientists, a woman who reaches age fifty-two today and remains free of cancer can expect to live to age ninety-two. Author Gail Sheehy writes, "People now have three adult lives to plan for; a provisional adulthood from 18 to 30; a first adulthood from about 30 to the mid-40s and a second adulthood from about 45 into the 80s." She says that the key to mastering this passage is to do something people generally haven't done before, which is to *plan* for this second adulthood.

It's heartening to know that other women have philosophical thoughts about aging. There's a broad range of expectation, capability, and emotional experience in aging—what is true for one person may not be true for another. The voices of the women in the following quotes are some of my favorites and will give you an idea of the diversity of experiences at the various ages and stages of a woman's life.

Fifty to Sixty Years Old

Old folks today are doing more than anyone ever thought they could. Why, when we were children, folks were knocking on death's door after turning fifty. Sixty was ancient.

—SARAH L. DELANY, *ON MY OWN AT 107*

Sixty to Seventy Years Old

Sixty years bring with them the privilege of discernment and vision: a capacity to behold, in the blink of an eye, the sweeping panorama of a life fully lived.

—CATHLEEN ROUNTREE, *ON WOMEN TURNING 60: EMBRACING THE AGE OF FULFILLMENT*

Seventy to Eighty Years Old

When I think that I'm seventy-eight, I think—how could that be? I just don't feel like whatever I would have thought seventy-eight would feel like. I just feel like myself.

—BETTY FRIEDAN, *LIFE SO FAR*

Eighty to Ninety Years Old

I am more and more aware of how important the framework is, what holds life together in a workable whole as one enters real old age, as I am doing. A body without bones would be an impossible

mess, so a day without a steady routine would be disruptive
and chaotic.

— MAY SARTON, *AT EIGHTY-TWO: A JOURNAL*

Ninety to One Hundred-Plus Years Old

Yes, being over ninety is different. . . . I can say with all honesty,
I'd rather be a very old woman than a very young one.

— REBECCA LATIMER, *YOU'RE NOT OLD UNTIL YOU'RE NINETY*

Somewhere along the line I made up my mind I'm going to live,
Bessie. I guess I probably don't have that much longer on this
Earth, but I may as well make the best of it.

— SARAH L. DELANY, *ON MY OWN AT 107*

Which quote do you relate to the most? Write a quote of your own
in your journal.

AGING IS ANOTHER COUNTRY

Actually, aging, after fifty, is an exciting new period; it is
another country.

— GLORIA STEINEM

We've never had the real possibility of living beyond a hundred years.
To be truthful, there are days when that prospect excites me. Is it possible that I may have more time to realize a few of my dreams, finish
reading all the books I bought, make new friends, have new adventures, repair screwed-up relationships, and organize (once and for all)
my front hall closet?

Then there are the days when the thought of one hundred (or even
ninety) gives me the willies. All that sagging skin, all those dead friends,

all those lost umbrellas and gloves, pills to take, young know-it-all doctors to undress for, insurance and Medicare forms to fill out.

I'm in a constant debate with myself: should I age into decrepitude or call the cosmic taxi for a fast ride to the Other Side while I still have gray matter that functions, while I still look and feel pretty good? We must all plan and prepare to live long, healthy, and productive lives. So perhaps we should keep our hearts and minds open to ways we can debunk the myths, fight the worn-out stereotypes—become warriors of a kind. I think about being a warrior, and I want to take a nap. Then I shift to a burning curiosity that asks the question, what will that "other country" that Gloria Steinem refers to have in store for me? And for heaven's sake, as I prepare for my trip there, what will my passport picture look like?

What are you going to do with your bonus years?

AN ATTITUDE OF GRATITUDE

The image in your mirror may be a little disappointing, but if you are still functioning and not in pain, gratitude should be the name of the game.

—BETTY WHITE

Self-help gurus have lectured to us about gratitude for years now. How much more harping are we willing to endure before we take their advice to heart? They're right, you know. Gratitude for even the smallest of things can magically shift a tough day from gray to sunny bright just like that.

Here is a case in point. I wake up mopey, eyes crusty, hair sticking up at right angles, the result of a crummy night's sleep. Groaning, I slide out of bed. Barefooted and stiff, I slog across the icy kitchen floor, reach for the coffeepot, realizing as I lift it that I've forgotten to set it up the night before. Now I must endure the noisy coffee bean grinder, put the coffee into the filter, pour water up to the line. It feels like three weeks until the damn java trickles into the pot. I desperately need my sanity, my caffeine. There is no joy in my life at this moment.

Then, like the GPS voice that says, "Recalculating," I get back on the right road. I remember the self-help gurus and decide to be grateful. I decide to focus on the positive, like author Ruth Turk who wrote, "To my amazement, I continue to find each decade of my lifetime more rewarding and exciting than the preceding ones." Let's see—I'm grateful I have a husband (snoring and all). I'm grateful I have a house and a warm bed to sleep in. I'm grateful for my sticky kitchen floor, and I'm grateful the floor is cold because it reminds me that I've forgotten my slippers (which I'm very grateful I have). I'm grateful for my coffeemaker and the aroma of freshly ground beans. And I'm thankful for the nose that enables me to smell the coffee brewing.

Got the idea? You can spend the day grousing because you forgot why you walked into the living room or you can be grateful for the legs that got you there.

Write about what you're grateful for today.

AN ATTITUDE OF SOLITUDE

It took some hard lessons for me to learn that I needed to be what I had thought was selfish; that I needed to take time to myself to write, to go to the brook, to be.

—Madeleine L'Engle

I remember coming upon my eighty-nine-year-old grandmother sitting in a chair, a tranquil look on her face. When I asked if she was okay, she said she was reliving a wonderful time in her younger years. At that time, Grandma still led a busy life—seeing friends, going to her club, listening to recorded books, caring for her grandchildren. Yet she knew how to be still. She was comfortable with solitude.

I was once afraid of solitude, afraid of my internal thoughts. As I age, I find I need time to be in touch with quiet me. Twitter, Facebook, Skype, cell phones, and email can put us in constant touch with each other but not necessarily in touch with ourselves. I now make a real effort to set aside time to get away from all of it. I have a need to know myself, to sort things out, to regroup. I want to understand how I think and feel and where I want to go with my life. I've come to realize that my need to pull away from other people is as universal as the urge to connect.

Time alone in quiet will serve to restore your integrity, allow you to think about your beliefs and what you value most. A self-imposed quiet can fertilize your creative side as ideas emerge, long buried by the daily noise and rush. Alone time replenishes energy, so when you resume interacting with others, you do so with renewed insight and strength.

Don't wait until you have a whole day or week free to incorporate a bit of solitude and reflection into your day. Walk in the park, sit in a room and listen to music, sink into a warm bath, meditate for ten minutes, or pet your cat. If you aren't used to being alone, you might feel a little bored at first. Stay with it. After a few tries, you may like it.

How can you create more solitude and quiet in your life?

BIRTHDAYS

If things get better with age, then you're approaching magnificent.

—NICOLE BEALE

Just before my fiftieth birthday, I suffered a concussion and damage to my neck in a car accident and consequently missed having the celebratory party I had envisioned. When I finally started to feel well enough to give a party (it took two years), I decided I would celebrate my fiftieth at age fifty-two. Now when my birthday rolls around, I feel each birthday is once again my fiftieth because, having survived that accident, I'm so glad to be alive.

I plan to celebrate my fiftieth over and over until I'm one hundred. I will never deny my true age, but when I send out the invitations to my birthday party each year, they will say, *I am celebrating my fiftieth again,* because that was the year I realized how precious and precarious life can be.

Gifts are another issue. Don't we have enough stuff at this point?! My eighty-year-old friend Alma suggested we should all get a hobby so our friends and our kids will know what to buy us. Then we won't end up with a bunch of extraneous nonsense. My friend Clarice told me, "When I turned fifty, I asked my husband to give me a gift that was older than me, and he gave me a bonsai tree!"

Negative feelings abound on the issue of birthdays. As author Mary McConnell says, "Turning sixty sneaks up on you, like a difficult guest you know is coming . . . and suddenly sixty knocks at the door." Some women I've spoken to barely enjoy their birthdays anymore. That's a shame, because for most, birthdays were so special when they were younger. Other women dread celebrating their birthdays because they don't like calling attention to their age.

Not everyone is negative when it comes to celebrating their years. On her sixtieth birthday, my friend Patty told me this, "On reaching sixty, I'm feeling a new freedom—total permission to be me. If I want to do anything, good or bad, the decision is totally mine. In recent years, I've rented a house on the beach where I celebrate my birthday with friends. My time at the beach house gives me a sense of peace and calm, and brings me back to who I am."

Try not to think too much about the accumulation of your birthdays and consider spending your birthday in a way that feels best to you—with others or alone. Or try one of these:

- Do something daring like rent a convertible and drive with the top down, or arrange for a hot air balloon ride.

- Throw yourself a party for an in-between birthday—like fifty-seven instead of sixty.

- Before your birthday, buy a beautiful journal. Fill every page with things you're proud of, and then give it to yourself as a birthday present.

- Spend part of the day meditating and reflecting on your life.

What would you like to do for your birthday this year?

SAYING WHAT I MEAN

Perhaps one can at last in middle age, if not sooner, be completely oneself. And what a liberation that would be!

—ANNE MORROW LINDBERGH

Gloria Steinem said, "Women may be the one group that grows more radical with age." Lynne Zielinski wrote, "Like autumn fruit, I've mellowed and thrown off inhibition to say what I mean." So has my sister, who wrote this poem:

Cookie Cutters

Aaaah, the scene opens . . .
whether you like it or not
rain punctuates puddles marking cadence
for a spotty spring ballet of fools
it's a goose-step two-step,
so very tiring especially if you do it right
I'm a sun-dancer with a tie-dye mind
running from clones in Cadillacs
drones in cathedrals, perpetually
harping we've fallen from grace
they're expecting the worst
and it never disappoints . . .
so many blank faces, so little time

how can anyone deny God's sense of humor
while under the sublime influence of Heaven
or is it advertising?
I declare war on snobbish university poets
their self-proclaimed perfectionism incensed
that we don't follow their rules,
their pentameters, particulars and perpendiculars
ha, you can't stop me now with your parameters,
there's a lot more where that came from
and I'm not about to do it your way
even if your power trip
IS bigger than I am
'cause I gotta voice

—Marilyn Houston

Listening to your inner voice makes it possible to start living more authentically—to speak with your own true voice and from your own system of values and beliefs. Telling it like it is invites women to go beyond the superficial injunctions of the culture, which tell us to be pleasant individuals, to be invisible or nice. As we age, it becomes even more important to assert our power in relationships and work. It's time to become more direct and more outspoken. We are entitled to feel wiser, less constrained by what others think. We become less judgmental and more capable of unconditional love—at the same time, we're tired of putting up with others' nonsense and unreasonable demands. We tell it like it is and have more of our authentic selves available to invest in friendships.

If you could broadcast a belief about a political, personal, or world issue that you haven't had the courage to express, what would it be? Write it out as a poem or a speech.

THE DECISION

People decide to get old. I've seen them do it. It's as if they've said, "Right, that's it, now I'm going to get old." Then they become old. Why they do this, I don't know.

—Doris Lessing

Perhaps you've entered a time in your life when your strength or abilities have diminished some. You were active in one pursuit or another your entire life, and now you're not as able to continue those activities. It's time to find a new purpose, a new reason for living, and it's time to find new opportunities that will cause you to stretch and grow. Where do you begin? Begin with a decision.

About fifteen years ago, I decided that I'm not aging—I'm evolving. I'm evolving and resolving not to get old. I plan to continue evolving until I die (and even beyond that, but that's another book).

If you must, decide to be old one day each year—the day you go for your physical and the doctor says, "You know, at your age, you should . . ." The other 364 days a year, when you're not in your doctor's office, put your energy into evolving. Here's another idea. Gather up all your health statistics (cholesterol numbers, and so on) and put them in a file. You know the statistics I'm talking about—those numbers that remind you that you're aging. Visit your statistics once a year or so (unless your health requires on another regimen) so you're aware of them but not fixated on them or what they signify. You have a choice—you can make the decision to put meaning and excitement into your life, or you can decide to get old.

What's your decision?

WAITING

The older one gets the more one feels that the present must be enjoyed; it is a precious gift, comparable to a state of grace.

—MARIE CURIE

As I age, I'm at the same time getting better at waiting and more impatient with it. When I barrel through my days at high speed, I'm increasingly aware that I miss the nuances of the moments that are only available when you are still.

I remember my grandmother, Grandma Agda. If someone was coming to take her out, she was always ready to go an hour ahead of time. She would sit patiently by the front door, coat on, purse held tightly on her lap, waiting. I felt uncomfortable seeing her sit there so long, but I now believe that it was a productive time for her and that she used those quiet, unhurried moments as an opportunity to be in the moment, to experience more fully what was happening inside and around her.

I want more slow time these days, more patience, more internal peace while I wait. When I was younger, waiting for anything made me anxious. I couldn't wait for Christmas, my birthday, to turn twelve, to turn twenty-one. I couldn't wait until graduation, until my baby was born, until the tulips came up, until summer arrived. I couldn't wait to get married, to buy a house, to receive the blouse I ordered, to go out on Saturday night.

I'm trying to slow down and live in the present. It becomes a balancing act between learning how to wait and not passively waiting for life to show up. Peaceful waiting means trusting that I am in the right place and that all is evolving in the universe as it was intended. So I wait, not for life to pass me by—but so that I can more clearly see life as it unfolds.

Sit quietly and bring yourself into the present with all its gifts.

part II

2
our self-image

Most important, I will learn that being old is a badge of honor, not a reason to hide in shame. I will refuse to be invisible!

—FINY HANSEN

With all the emphasis society places on appearance, the scariest part of aging for many women is that they have to rely more on who they are than on what they look like for respect and attention.

For some women, self-image and self-esteem begin to decline with age. They feel invisible. They feel young on the inside but not in their outward appearance. They find it takes more effort to maintain their looks and their bodies.

In the past, I could eat what I liked without gaining too much weight. Imagine my amazement when this metabolic miracle ended just as I was on the cusp of fifty. I felt estranged from my body, and the weight gain I experienced after menopause was weighing me down. I had to ask myself: am I so attached to my younger, thinner looks that now I've misplaced who I really am?

Sometimes I want to be like author Ruth Harriet Jacobs. Ruth likes to wear outrageous clothes. She writes, "I am a woman of size but refuse to hide in black or navy blue. I wear bright colors and wild styles rather than apologizing for age or taking up sizable space in the world."

Some of the older women in my neighborhood have white hair, some are arthritic and stooped, and some look like they've given up. Sometimes we smile at each other. But I wonder if they consider me one of their own. Or have I fooled them with my dyed hair, my cosmetics, and my gym clothes? Sometimes I feel like an impostor, and part of me wants to deny kinship with these older women. I want to be in the club, but I want to look good, feel good, and project health, too.

Should we totally ignore our looks? Of course not, but as older women, we are also much more. There are two authors whom I particularly admire for their insight and wisdom on this. Melody Beattie says, "Love how you look, smell, and feel. Love the color of your eyes, the color of your hair, and the radiance of your heart. . . . Love your mistakes, and love all the good you've done." Elizabeth Cady Stanton, a major figure in the women's rights movement of the 19th century once said, "Be kind, noble, generous, well-mannered, be true to yourselves and your friends, and the soft lines of these tender graces and noble virtues will reveal themselves in the face."

Stand before a mirror. Who do you see there? Not what, but *who?*

BECOMING INVISIBLE

Many women approaching 50 don't feel glamorous; they feel invisible. . . . I think they mean sexually invisible, but if they send out the right vibes, they won't be.

—Judith Krantz

You will develop very low self-esteem if you've relied on your looks to give you a sense of value. If you think that's the only way you are valued, then be prepared to be invisible and stay that way.

I remember the first time I heard the invisibility indictment. I was sitting with a client who was fifteen years older than I am, which made her about fifty-six at the time. She had just gone through the healing process from a difficult divorce and was ready to start dating for the first time in thirty years. She said she felt invisible and unnoticed at social events even when she was dressed well and coiffed to the nines. I recall thinking that I would never feel that way.

Well, I've come to feel some of the invisibility I was so sure I would never experience. I thought it would be more upsetting than it is. I thought my self-esteem would plummet and that I wouldn't feel sexy or desirable anymore. But as author Mary McConnell wrote, "Growing older is not a reason to develop low self-esteem. Many women find new confidence and self-assurance after fifty."

So I'm creating new confidence and self-assurance. I go to an aquasize class at the gym, and I watch what I eat. I've lost a few pounds and feel much better. I've also had my colors done, which is an analysis by an image consultant to find out what colors are best for me to wear, and a makeup consultation that is helping me to feel better about myself. Am I still invisible? Probably, maybe.

But I'm not invisible to me. I matter, and I'm here, on solid ground, feeling confident and in tune with my body. Author Marianne Williamson says, "As we age, gorgeous young hunks may or may not be interested in us any more. For that matter, men our own age and older might not be interested anymore. My response to that is 'so what?'"

Try saying to yourself: "I will arrive at the point where I am comfortable with who I am and with being as invisible as I choose to be."

What can you begin to do today to feel better about yourself?

YOU DON'T LOOK LIKE A GRANDMA!

There are more grandmothers alive today than at any other time in the history of the world. However, today's grandmothers don't look like grandmothers.

—LOIS WYSE

What's a grandmother supposed to look like? Mine looked sweet and had small, strong, arthritic hands. Her skin was transparent, and loose crepe-paper skin decorated her outstretched arms. Her eyes twinkled like Mrs. Santa Claus's, and when she got mad, her face reddened and her voice got my attention. After the scolding, she would give me a big hug, and then, wrapped in a handmade apron, she'd produce stacks of thin, buttery Swedish pancakes. Did she look like a grandma? You bet. More than that, in the best sense, she acted like one.

Grandma was the one you could go to with the stuff you didn't want to share with your mother. She wasn't as judgmental. Mine played cards—and Parcheesi and Chinese checkers—with us. She taught me how to sew with a thimble and how to knit scarves.

I have grandchildren. Do I look like a grandmother? I would like to think not—yet, what am I so worried about? I would like to be more of a grandmother and not as concerned about every little wrinkle, ache, and pain. I want to be the warm place the grandkids come to with their problems. I'd like to worry less about my weight and be more available to read them a book, play gin rummy, or join them in a video game. I'd like to be less concerned with how much the skin on my arms is sagging and to focus more on giving warm hugs.

What can you do to be less concerned about your appearance and more engaged with your grandchildren (or other family members)?

WHO IS THAT OLD WOMAN?

Sometimes I look in the mirror expecting to see the body, the face of my youth because I remember her. She's still in me.

—MELODY BEATTIE

One day in my mid-fifties, I woke up to the birds singing outside my window, and I could smell the coffee brewing. I believed it was going to be a perfect day until I struggled to my feet, hand on my back, and hobbled past the full-length mirror on the bedroom door. As I stared at my reflection, I remember thinking, *Who is that old woman? Am I still in there?*

Here's something else that just made my day—in doing research for this book, I read that after fifty, our tissues start drying out! This is one reason why weight can actually drop after fifty-five. And of all things, around sixty-five our noses and earlobes elongate. Floppy earlobes and long noses! However, our biological clocks tick at wildly different rates, and no two women will age in exactly the same way. So, while some of you are drying out and losing weight at age fifty-five, others of you may not experience nose droop until you're eighty.

I called my friend Deb for some consolation. She listened while I moaned and groaned about my issues with aging. She jokingly replied, "Let's just end it all and be done with it!" That's one way to put an end to your concern, but I think it's important to have a more upbeat approach. Don't you? I'm considering this: when my ears are longer, my dangle earrings will swing better, and if my nose gets longer, I won't have to stoop down as far to smell the flowers!

In your journal, write down some positive, encouraging statements about aging.

SAGGING FACES AND LIVER SPOTS

An 82-year-old friend of mine decided to buy herself some nips and tucks. Her daughter said that at her age it would just be rearranging the deck chairs on the Titanic.

—PEG BRACKEN

Sixty-two-year-old Mary told me, "I had a facelift and had those bags removed from under my eyes. So now my face looks as young as my body feels. Believe me, I'd do it again without hesitation." Thanks to cosmetic surgery, others don't have to see us as middle-aged or older. With special contact lenses, you'll never give away your age by needing your reading glasses to cut your steak. A little hair coloring from the box can "wash that gray right out of your hair," and advances in plastic surgery make it possible to erase years from your face and body. But as author Lois Wyse wrote, "As for cosmetic surgery, until they figure out a way to make a woman's hands look as young as her face—who's she kidding?"

These days, you can erase a decade from your looks if you choose to. The question is: how do you choose to live peacefully with your looks when the pressure to do just the opposite is so overwhelming?

Liver spots have nothing to do with your liver. Those flat, brownish spots are the result of years of sun exposure. They're bigger than freckles and appear on the faces, hands, and arms of fair-skinned people. That's me! The medical name for them is solar lentigo, but they're also called senile lentigo, not because you're getting senile but because the name comes from the Latin word for "old." Senile liver spots!

I think we make ourselves miserable. At a certain point in our lives, we find ourselves engaged in fighting back against every ounce of weight gain or every hint of a wrinkle. We engage in countless efforts to hold back the ravages of time until finally, at some point, we give up and forget about the whole thing. That's when we become happy again. Even sagging faces look beautiful when adorned with a smile. And liver spots? Oh heck, call them freckles if it makes you feel better.

Are you too obsessed with looking young, or are you doing just enough to feel good about yourself?

HIGH MAINTENANCE

I want to grow old without facelifts. . . . I want to have the courage to be loyal to the face I've made.

—MARILYN MONROE

Despite my usual optimistic outlook, I've collided with age and its required upkeep. I wish I could report that I arrived at these high-maintenance years with complete grace and dignity, but that's not true. If I want to, I can dress like a teenager, inject collagen into my wrinkles, color away the gray hairs, replace my old dry nails with acrylics, and liposuction the belly rolls. But thinking about all of this makes me just plain tired!

Do you find yourself examining your skin for possible melanomas? They look like brown or black, crusty, irregular-shaped growths that show up from nowhere as you age. It's a good idea to have your skin checked by a dermatologist once in a while. But try not to obsess about every little bump. What about that cellulite? I don't think any amount of maintenance can cure that. Just don't look in the three-way mirror in the dressing room anymore.

Have you noticed that the heroines of your favorite movies are discreetly, yet beautifully, older women and that they just keep looking better? Well, consider that it's part of their job to maintain themselves and that they've got thousands of dollars of income to spend on themselves. So go easy on yourself, and try to enjoy a beautiful maintenance-free day once in a while.

What can you stop obsessing about so much?

FEELING YOUNG INSIDE

I am not young but I feel young. The day I feel old, I will go to bed and stay there.

—Coco Chanel

Some older women I've met say, "I feel much younger than I look. I'm not aging on the inside." I think we've all had that feeling at one time or another. I see photographs of myself or recordings of TV programs I've appeared on, and I can't relate to the images I see. I feel so much younger than I look. May Sarton wrote in her journal, *At Seventy,* "Seventy must seem extremely old to my young friends, but I actually feel much younger than I did . . . six years ago."

Regardless of what the outside looks like, inner beauty is a beacon, like a beam of light that reveals something undeniable about a woman's core. So what is this light? I believe it's the ability to experience pleasure that makes a woman desirable and beautiful. Pleasure in her work, in her friends, in the food she eats, maybe even pleasure in her stressful days. Isn't it a woman's unconscious pleasure in herself and others that allows her to lean forward and let go, and make the rest of us want to lean in toward her, wanting to connect?

The older woman with inner beauty knows this, and she is resolute. She has made tough choices to become who she is. We appear much more beautiful and youthful to others if we can say, "Here I am, with all my flaws, passions, and vices." Show me inner beauty, and I'll show you a woman who has rid herself of the superfluous, both inside and out, who has kept what she needs, refused the rest, and regretted nothing. This culling, often called centering, is at the heart of every system of spiritual enlightenment I know of, and the result is what finally accounts for inner beauty's insistent glow.

Several coats of black mascara and a little concealer won't interfere with your spiritual life; I promise. Even the most evolved among us still has to face the day. We make a mistake if we see inner beauty and outer beauty as somehow antithetical, demanding that inner loveliness stand on its own without even moisturizer or a bit of blush. Self-nurturance doesn't negate self-worth but rather bolsters it.

If beauty comes from the core, then what part do our looks play? Should we just nurture and support our inner selves and forget about the outer? Are the two, as we sometimes fear, mutually exclusive?

OLD BODIES, NEW AGAIN

You don't get to choose how you're going to die, or when. You can only decide how you're going to live now.

—Joan Baez

Even if you've never exercised or eaten right, you can start now. But I don't want to be one more nagging expert telling you to exercise and get in shape. Let me just tell you my story instead. At fifty-four years old and five feet nine inches, I weighed in at a hefty 236 pounds. Too much Kozy Shack pudding, Raisinets, and Rice Krispies Treats, and a lot of sitting around on my duff. I joined Weight Watchers and the gym and lost thirty pounds. While it was an improvement, I was starting to think this old body could never feel new again.

Now I'm in my sixties, five feet eight inches (I lost an inch somewhere!), and still struggle with my weight, but I go to an aquasize class three times a week, and I feel much younger and full of energy.

Our muscles have memory (thank goodness some part of me has memory). If you exercise regularly and then stop—even for years—your muscles will respond more quickly when you start exercising again than the muscles of someone who never exercised.

When it comes to taking control of your physical self, I like what actress Helen Hayes once said: "If you look at all the assembled data on the decline of the human body, you'll come to the inevitable conclusion that you are, if not in command, certainly in charge of supervising how you age."

It's important to get out and find some exercise you enjoy. Remember that even an old body can feel new again. It doesn't matter how long you've had negative thoughts about your body—you can begin to make a change today.

What steps can you take toward a healthier body?

PROUD OF OUR WRINKLES

Growing older is a nice feeling. It's something people don't talk about. They only talk about wrinkles.

—Isabella Rossellini

Many women are fearful of looking older and are willing to put up with the pain and expense to look as young as they feel. In this country, cosmetic surgery has increased by 75 percent in recent years.

So you want to laser away wrinkles, lift those droopy eyelids, or tighten that turkey gobbler neck? You can share your retirement money with a plastic surgeon to get a few tucks around your eyes or chin or both. Or you could invest in some expensive magic cream that manufacturers proclaim will erase your wrinkles. Not me. I'm kind of proud of my wrinkles—wrinkles that say I've struggled hard to be a good mother, an aunt, a grandmother; that I've taken pride in my home, my garden, my ability to keep ten plates in the air; that I've worked hard to become a successful author, a gardener, a baker of bread, a singer, and a therapist.

My wrinkles are the stripes that represent my years of service. Each one represents a laugh, a sorrow, a struggle, a ray of sunshine, or a concern for another. Plus, they get me a seat on the bus and a discount at the movies!

Botox and collagen injections, laser treatments, chemical peels, and dermabrasion are all attempts to erase the real beauty and intelligence of the aging face. Our facial lines show that we've lived. I admire the character and intelligence of faces that are no longer youthful. The intelligence of a mature face is much more compelling than the insipid beauty of someone whose main asset is a tight face with no crow's-feet.

Older, grayer women than you are spending their facelift money on going back to school, paying for a massage or yoga classes, and taking trips to Australia to watch the sunrise.

I find myself studying the slightly crinkly eyes of my older friends as I try to develop some appreciation for my own fine lines. I also refuse to compare myself with other women of any age. Instead of trying to look young, I'm aiming for being unique.

What does your face say about you?

LOOKING GOOD

Even when you know you'll be completely alone for a day or more, put on your makeup, comb your hair, and dress in something comfortable, but nice-looking. . . . It makes you feel good.

—"Judge Judy" Sheindlin

My friend Sari Martin, a professional personal image coach, says, "No matter what your age, plan an event every day for which you need to get dressed—a trip to the grocery store or post office, a walk with a grandchild, or tea with a friend. Women can get lazy, especially after they retire, and end up wearing their bathrobe for half the day or slipping on a pair of sweatpants and a loose t-shirt. Loose-fitting clothing affects your posture and the way you walk, and it negatively impacts your energy. Making the effort to get dressed says you feel good about yourself."

I think the key to looking good and feeling good as you grow older is to keep trying new things—new hairstyles, wardrobe colors, exercises, even foods. Do some experimenting, and enjoy the results. See a professional about your makeup. Ask for advice on a makeover. Try some different looks, and see which suits you best.

Pay attention to which colors brighten your complexion and which ones leave you looking washed out. How about a new perfume? Try two or three different fragrances. Switching scents will make you feel fresh and different. A facial massage will help your face look more relaxed. For heaven's sake, get a pedicure. A pedicure, complete with a foot and leg massage, relaxes you and makes you look and feel special right down to your toes.

It's unfortunate that we're bombarded with so many images of perfection. But even so, it seems some of our celebrities have the right idea. Consider what actress Isabella Rossellini said, "I don't do anything to look younger. . . . It is more becoming to accept the unique characteristics that come with age. Women who stay true to themselves are always more interesting and beautiful."

World-famous model Iman said in an interview, "After a certain age, thinness is not attractive. . . . Five extra pounds can make you look healthier, younger, more attractive." Laura Mercier, renowned makeup artist, says, "Age is sexy because it brings wisdom and knowledge of yourself. As for style, you know what looks good on you. You've learned from your past mistakes; you are not distracted by trends."

Let's face it—you look good when you are comfortable with who you are. That's what shows, and that's what makes you beautiful.

What can you do to feel more confident and relaxed about how you look?

NOW WHO AM I?

I love being old . . . because I am more myself than I have ever been.

—MAY SARTON

As my grandmother aged, her life became less about what she looked like and more about who she was becoming. I hope I'm like her. I want this second half of my life to bring with it a different dimension of growth from the first half.

If you're trying way too hard to stay young, you may be stalling out your own self-discovery. Have you accepted that you're in life's second half but still struggle with the unanswered question: now who am I?

In trying to answer that question, you may be so terrified that you attempt to make superficial changes to your old persona while avoiding any profound inner change or self-understanding.

Suzanne, a sixty-year-old artist and writer, told me, "I'm not going to apologize for my age. I'm going to wear my hair long and gray if I want to just because it feels good. I intend to feel my feelings and think my thoughts. I am who I am."

Perhaps you've had the experience of suddenly realizing that the structure of your life does not seem to fit you and you don't know why. Relationships you chose may now seem unfulfilling. Your aging face suddenly seems prominent. Material things that once brought pleasure may now seem totally inadequate. A lifestyle that once seemed satisfying or tolerable now grates on your nerves. Goals that were clear may become overwhelming or blurred. You may change the old mask cosmetically, buy new clothes, or change your hairstyle. But something is going on inside that you can't deny. You can't sort of begin this quest. Either you do, or you don't—the time to decide has arrived.

For some women, their identity was wrapped up solely in their love relationships or in being a mother. In accommodating themselves to others and focusing on others, many women neglect building a sense of themselves as distinct and valuable individuals. Have you lost yourself in a long-term relationship or marriage? Is your self-esteem dependent on how your mate feels about you? If you spent half your life focusing on him or your children so much that you don't know what your own wants, needs, and desires are, it's now time to commit to being more authentic. At midlife, a woman's most obvious sense of herself may be in terms of her relationships with others as daughter, wife, mother, or employee. When she realizes this, the question of who she is apart from these relationships is a challenge to answer.

You may be fifty and already deeply engaged in the quest, or you may be eighty and still resisting it. This is because your chronological age is based on clock time; the quest moves through soul time, which many people encounter for the first time only in life's second half. Soul time has less to do with calendars than with the deepest dimensions of life.

Author Ruth Raymond Thone says, "As an aging woman, I must give myself permission to be who I am, even if that is not culturally approved or productive. . . . I want to affirm who I am at each moment of my life, not wishing for another time, another self, nor molding myself to fit an inner shape that no longer serves." In this second half of your life, you have another chance, another opportunity to go deeper, to learn who you are now.

How would you define yourself at this age?

STRONG IN A YOUTH-OBSESSED WORLD

Atomic Mother

I'm here now to tell it like it is,
in spite of your arrogance, your ignorance.
Love and determination keep me strong
in a youth-obsessed world that doubts my value.
I refuse your chronic misperceptions, definitions
that try to keep me small and powerless.
Classic Mother, that's not all I am, I promise you.
Simple acts of love revealed my power
even before I held the universe in my womb.
I've given all to those I love, so don't assume
my gender renders me diminished.
At any given hour, I'd kill or give my life for them,
the ones I love—without hesitation.
I've got a strength that goes beyond your understanding.
Should I not be seen as Goddess in your eyes?
Is my power to create too much for you to bear?
Am I less than clever for the wrinkles on my face?
Am I less than the shadow of your perfection?
Take a look at your own reflection
. . . and your lies.

—MARILYN HOUSTON

Women of the 1960s and 1970s were forerunners and barrier break-ers. As a group, we pioneer women (both working women and stay-at-home wives and mothers) were joined by others who felt exhausted and vacuous. We had courage in the face of resentment, we stood up to be shunned and satirized. We were some of the first women to rescue ourselves instead of waiting for the knight on the white horse.

How to do you feel about Marilyn Houston's poem "Atomic Mother"?

What can you do to feel stronger and more confident about your self-image and about the person you have become?

3
our minds

Our sweetest life, our truest life, is with us always—beyond the senses, ever rooted in consciousness.

—MARSHA SINETAR

As the nation's baby boomers age, the number of Americans with late-life mental or emotional issues is expected to climb. Millions of women over fifty already struggle with the changes, losses, and stresses of growing older, and their numbers are increasing.

Put simply, I don't want to lose my mind—or my way home for that matter. It reassures me to know that some mental challenges such as depression, chronic anxiety, and dementia are not part of normal aging and can be addressed. We've had a revolution in our understanding of the brain, and we now know that the brain is constantly rebuilding itself throughout life. More good news—the past few decades have seen the emergence of a full-fledged specialty in medicine called geriatric psychiatry, aimed specifically at the diagnosis and treatment of mental and emotional problems that affect older people.

Researchers in neuroscience and psychology are continuing to discover more about the nature of consciousness, memory, emotions, creativity, dreams, and other mental phenomena as well as how and why the brain ages. Their answers suggest that some of these mysteries may be largely solved within our lifetimes.

YOUR BRAIN IS A MUSCLE

Women who believe in themselves are enhanced by the sum of their years. We are repositories of the experience and wisdom of our time.

—Betty Nickerson

A once-common notion that the brain declines with age is completely false. Scientists have demonstrated that new brain cells can actually be generated in adults, proving that the brain continues to grow and actually improves with age. Until very late in life, older people tend to perform better than younger ones in certain areas, such as vocabulary, numerical skills, spatial orientation, and interpersonal problem solving.

The brain is like any other muscle in the body, and it must be exercised to stay in shape. Since the brain depends on the cardiovascular system to supply it with oxygen-rich blood, it is crucial to remain physically active as you age. Lack of physical exercise is likely more responsible than age itself for declining brain function.

Besides physical exercise, an unfit brain can be whipped back into shape with a program for the brain called neurobic exercise that encourages you to try different things and develop new hobbies. Here is a sample list of fun things you can do, pulled from *Keep Your Brain Alive* by Lawrence C. Katz, PhD:

- Take a different route to work.

- Turn pictures on your desk upside down.

- Shop for food at an ethnic market.

- Sit in a different seat at the dinner table.

Getting Older Better

- Have a blind wine tasting. (I like this one!)

- Go camping.

Take care of your health, and your brain will love you for it! Eat a nutritious, balanced diet. B_6, B_{12}, and folic acid are particularly important for memory, as are the antioxidant vitamins C and E and beta-carotene. Have regular checkups, too, because memory problems can be caused by cardiovascular conditions; thyroid dysfunction; depression; diabetes; lung, liver, or kidney problems; and drug side effects. See your eye doctor as well, because changes in sight or vision can contribute to memory problems.

What steps do you want to take to care for your brain?

SENIOR MOMENTS

Losing our minds is more frightening to most of us than death.

—Sallirae Henderson

Don't you just hate it when you find yourself standing in the middle of a room saying, "Now what was I on my way to do?" Author Mary C. Morrison wrote, "It takes longer to remember things. . . . But if we wait—a name, a place, an event will come to mind, swimming slowly to the surface, like a fish rising." That reminds me of the day I wanted to remember to bring up fish for dinner from the basement freezer. I wrote the word *FISH* on a sticky note and stuck it to the front of my t-shirt. When my assistant showed up later that day, she had a good laugh when she saw the note still stuck to my shirt and no fish defrosting in the kitchen. Not only had I forgotten about the fish, I had completely forgotten about the note as well. Talk about fish rising slowly!

Memory is composed of a collection of dendrites, or neurological connections, that make up an organic function subject to injury or atrophy. Not all memory lapses are normal. See your doctor if you forget things much more often than you used to—like how to do things you have often done before, get lost in familiar places, forget where you've been for a few hours, have substantial trouble learning new things, lose awareness of daily events, or start to repeat phrases or anecdotes during the same conversation.

Simple memory lapses are probably not due to a biological problem, so lighten up on yourself. In our many years on this planet, we've stored a great deal of information in our noggins. Frankly, we need to let go of some in order to make room for more.

Try not to judge yourself when a senior moment happens. If you're worried, tell your doctor what's going on. In the meantime, decorate yourself with sticky notes in bright colors to match your outfits and accept that a metaphorical fish will slip through your fingers from time to time.

What changes or devices can you implement to help you remember things?

MIND-BODY CONNECTION

> *My body has been giving me strong hints for some time now that things are changing. . . . It's the mind that's so reluctant to accept the phenomenon of aging.*
>
> —B. J. BATEMAN

My friend Alma told me, "Don't say, 'I must be getting older' because your body hears you, and then it reacts that way." Alma's right. Scientists have developed new molecular and pharmacological tools that have made it possible to identify the intricate communication network that exists between the immune system and the brain, a network that allows the two systems to signal each other continuously and rapidly. These systems guard against infectious, inflammatory, autoimmune, and associated mood disorders. These systems also hear everything we say.

What we think about pain also has an effect on the amount of pain we're in. I remember reading about a 102-year-old woman who said that she had a pain in her finger and decided it might be arthritis. She said to her finger, "If you're trying to attack me with arthritis, nothing doing!" She started thinking positively, massaged her finger every day, and a couple of months later, her arthritis pain was gone.

How old would I be if I didn't know how old I was? I'm not sure, but I think I'm around forty-five. If my body keeps getting messages from my mind such as: "I'm too old to walk that far," "I'm not young anymore," "Women my age don't do that," then I take the risk that my mind is going to hear me and my body is going to obey. Watch what you tell yourself about aging—your body is listening.

In your journal, write out some positive affirmations you will say to your mind and body each day.

LOSING THINGS

You can decline to look for items you misplace. Let them find you.

—Peg Bracken

I don't think losing things is necessarily a result of the weakened cognitive abilities that come with age. We lose things primarily because we don't pay attention to where we're putting them in the first place. When I'm intent on remembering where I've put something, I say out loud to myself, "I'm putting the car keys on the dresser." Saying aloud where I've put something has been shown to create the necessary neural pathway for retrieval later. I don't care if anyone hears me talking to myself. Those listening may think I've gone crazy, but talking to myself is better than going nuts trying to find things.

Another way I help myself keep track of things is designating what organizers call a landing spot. My spot is on the dining room table where I put anything that has to go with me in the car when I do my errands; that's where I put mail to go out, my keys, my cell phone, my purse, and the bag for the Goodwill bin. One woman I know places everything she wants to remember to take with her directly in front of the door so she can't get out without tripping on her stuff.

Losing things doesn't mean you're getting old and losing your mind. You just need to pay attention, develop a system, and put things back in the same place each time.

What system of keeping track of things would work best for you?

IS IT MENOPAUSE OR MENTAL PAUSE?

During menopause we are literally moving into our wisdom years, where we can access a broader range of knowledge and can synthesize things rationally.

—Christiane Northrup, MD

Among the menopause-related topics we hesitate to discuss is the feeling that our brains have gone soft. Some women worry that their intelligence is diminishing because their thinking has become foggy or sluggish. *Foggy* and *fuzzy thinking* emerged as terms of reference in the 1990s to describe the sometimes confused thought processes that many women experience during menopause.

Doctors may dismiss memory loss and difficulty concentrating as a result of stress or, in menopausal women, low estrogen levels. But those symptoms can also mean you have hypothyroidism (underactive thyroid) or that you are depressed. Both can have an effect on the brain and can be treated effectively, so it's best to have a full physical to check on these things.

Medical textbooks say estrogen appears to function as a mild vasodilator to increase blood flow within the brain. As a woman transitions through menopause, according to documented research, the actions of estrogen on neurotransmitters and receptors in the brain change.

Some good news: It appears that certain processes and functions of the brain make permanent shifts after menopause so that many women become more creative later in life because the parts of their brains that handle creativity become more active! So take life a little slower at this time, create something, and take action to ease your mind.

What are you willing to do to ease your mind?

MEMORY, WHAT MEMORY?

There is one anxiety about aging that I think we could well do without, and that is when we can't remember a name, or can't recall what it is we have started to do. . . . It does not mean we are getting senile.

—Eda LeShan

You may find your memory is not as good as it used to be. All is not lost, though, including your memory. There are a number of simple strategies to keep your memory working to capacity and your mind sharp. Aerobic exercises can improve memory by 20 percent or more. Use to-do lists and sticky notes, of course. Get enough sleep. Keep your stuff organized or reduce the amount of stuff you've got to keep track of. That should help a lot. Remember to keep your stress in check. Hormones released under stress interfere with the brain's ability to remember detailed information.

Here's an interesting find—research says people age seventy and older performed better on memory tests than others did. A battery of tests was done, and they discovered that the greatest improvements were found among people in their eighties and those who had never graduated from high school!

Saint-Exupéry said that in our old age we will sit under the sheltering branches of the tree of our memories. I just love that image—now if I could just remember who Saint-Exupéry is!

What steps can you take to bolster your memory?

CONTINUED LEARNING

As you get older . . . the trick is to continue to learn, to challenge yourself.

—HELEN HAYES

One of the best ways to keep your brain healthy is to take some classes, either at a university or by enrolling in a local continuing education program. You may hesitate about going to school because you'll feel old enough to be the mother or grandmother of your classmates. Don't worry about them. You are entitled to learn and grow at every stage in your life. In fact, I've heard younger students say how inspired they were by older people in their classes.

Have you heard about Elderhostel, creator of Road Scholar? At the time of this writing, it's the world's largest educational travel organization for people age fifty-five and older. There are 5,500 Elderhostel programs in 150 countries. The instructors are professionals, and the accommodations are usually high quality.

Some universities and colleges offer scholarships for adults who want to return to school, so check out that possibility. Schools also are known to waive the requirements for certain classes if you can demonstrate your life experience or professional background is similar to the course's curriculum.

You could get a degree online or take yourself to a class. I think it may be more stimulating to attend a class with other students if you can. The class discussions can be the most interesting part of the learning experience, and you may make some new friends in the process.

Have you put a dream or passion on hold because you didn't have the skills or education? Perhaps you put off college or pursuing additional training while you raised your children or supported your husband. Now it's your turn. Take the chance to rethink your future, to listen to that still, small voice within you—the voice that has, from time to time, whispered a dream to your heart.

Do you think going to school is a good idea for you? If so, what would you like to study?

BRAIN GROWTH

If I manage to learn something new, I glow with a pleasure that life seldom gave me in youth, when I took all of this for granted.

—MARY C. MORRISON

Society's knowledge doubles about every ten years, thanks in part to Internet resources, and the average person today has already absorbed five to ten times the knowledge and experience of their grandparents. I say that knowing five to ten times what my grandparents knew is quite enough, thank you. And I suppose we could just stop there, not learn anything new, and be content knowing what we know. But as I age I don't want my brain to stop growing altogether, so I've made a decision to keep it stimulated and challenged.

Older people score higher than younger people on some mental tests. The theory is that older folks make fewer errors because the age-related decline in memory function makes them less likely to be led astray by misleading contextual information. Ha ha, younger people—we win!

I've got some ideas. Try one of these brain-growing activities to enjoy your life more:

- Learn photography or a foreign language.

- Memorize a poem.

- Learn to play a musical instrument.

- Play games (chess and Scrabble are great for the brain) or learn new ones.

- Read some great literature.

- Redecorate your environment.

- Try solving crossword puzzles (start with the easy ones) or Sudoku.

What actions will you take to keep your brain growing and active?

4
our emotions

People with positive outlooks . . . who marshal their energies to defeat creeping depression or entropy, are far more likely to extend their Second Adulthoods into satisfying later lives.

—GAIL SHEEHY

By about fifty, we've amassed a hoard of wisdom that should carry us through the rest of our lives. But too often, difficult emotions get in the way, and accessing our stored wisdom becomes a challenge. We may lose our optimism for life to bouts of situational depression. Losses begin to pile up as we age. We are challenged to keep our emotions stable and, fighting for our lost youth, we forget how to yield gracefully.

In addition to the normal aging process, other factors, such as health, influence our emotional lives. The condition of your health will have an effect on how much you do in your life, how you do it, and how you function emotionally. If you focus on and build on the strengths you do have, your emotional life will be less affected, and aging will become more satisfying. The emotional aspect of aging is a challenge, but it's an opportunity for enormous growth. Happiness as you age is not just a matter of good health and a high standard of living. It's also a matter of feeling in control of your environment.

BAD MOODS

Tears do come occasionally into one's eyes . . . and no matter what invisible wound they seep from, they purge and heal.

—M. F. K. FISHER

Who hasn't had a bad mood? Moods seem to show up like an ambush, unannounced, uninvited, and unprovoked. Often moods are tied to a particular circumstance, such as your gray roots growing back before you've had a chance to buy more hair color, forgetting to pay your credit card bill, or not having enough cash to pay it, or looking in the mirror to find your cellulite is dropping toward your knees. Other common sources that trigger bad moods include illness, loneliness, boredom, unrealistic expectations, and failure to accomplish a goal.

Bad moods certainly magnify the trivial annoyances of life. Like running out of tea bags or coffee filters, forgetting your toast in the toaster, and tripping over the cat while looking for your glasses (for the seventh time). On the other hand, the unprovoked moods are the most annoying, I think. It's much easier when we can blame something or someone for the mood we're in—however, it's not always a kind or helpful thing to do.

Take time to analyze what was happening before the bad mood occurred because this may give you a clue to the remedy. Keep a mood journal where you track your ups and downs for a while. Note the circumstances (where you were, with whom, and what you were doing). Try to catch and record the internal events that preceded them—thoughts, memories, fantasies. You can take your journal to your doctor or a therapist if you think your bad moods are making you more depressed and getting in the way of enjoying your life.

You can try one of the following to help ease your mood:

- Shift the focus away from your bad mood by doing something for someone else.

- Eat a little bit of chocolate. (I prefer walnut fudge.) It prompts the release of serotonin, the brain's natural chemical upper. Eat it slowly, savoring the sweetness and texture.

- Play with a toy. Two of my favorites are Slinky and Play-Doh. Something as simple as a yo-yo or a windup toy can help distract your mind and relax your body.

- Take a quick walk. Walking prompts the release of endorphins and provides a change of scenery that may distract you from your problems. One of my personal favorites is walking in the woods with an inexpensive bottle of bubble soap in hand, blowing bubbles as I go.

- Listen to upbeat music—rock, heavy metal, rap, reggae, ragtime (my seventy-year-old sister loves Metallica!). Sing along to the music; belt it out—it helps.

- Ask friends to help cheer you up or allow their positive outlook to infect you. Avoid people who bring you down.

In your journal, write about some things you've done in the past that have helped pull you out of a bad mood.

IS IT SADNESS OR DEPRESSION?

One was happy at one moment, unhappy two minutes later, and neither for any good reason; so what did it mean?

—V. Sackville-West

The World Health Organization claims that depression, although higher in women, falls dramatically after sixty-five years of age. Hooray! Another benefit of growing older is that we are growing less depressed.

Even so, are you finding that you've lost your usual spark and sense of humor? Have you stopped going out? Are you avoiding your friends? Do you stare dully at the TV? Do even the grandkids fail to cheer you up? You might tell yourself that it's just a passing mood, but there could be another reason. Serious depression is a draining condition that can ruin the quality of life and often goes unrecognized in older people.

Clinical depression is more than sadness, the blues, or a reaction to grief. Depression is a medical problem, like hypertension or diabetes, and the condition isn't a part of normal aging. A large percentage of depressed older women don't get relief because they are reluctant to seek help or because their doctors don't readily recognize this issue. Doctors often miss the diagnosis because their depressed older patients usually see them for physical complaints instead.

Minor depression usually lifts on its own. But you're likely to need active measures to banish a lingering case. As a first step, get adequate sleep, eat a nourishing diet, and spend more time with friends and family. Exercise is also a powerful antidote. In more persistent cases, therapy can reveal the underlying causes of depression, help reverse negative attitudes, and find better ways of handling problems. For some people, antidepressant medication can also help.

Some of the symptoms of depression that warrants treatment are: feeling worthless, empty, unloved, hopeless; no longer enjoying things; feeling very tired and lethargic, nervous, restless, or irritable; being unable to concentrate; crying frequently; sleeping more or less than usual; having persistent headaches, stomachaches, or pain; and in extreme cases, having thoughts of death, especially suicide. If you are having thoughts of suicide, *tell someone and seek immediate help.*

Generally, psychiatrists believe most depression is biochemical, but many of them don't accept a specific link between hormone deficiency and depression. Women with obvious hormonal issues are sometimes treated with antidepressants. In these cases, the underlying hormonal component of their depression is often misdiagnosed.

Sudden depression in someone over age fifty may signal a silent stroke. Silent strokes don't result in classic stroke symptoms (severe headache, dizziness, and loss of motor skills) but are often the precursor to a full stroke. Some may have subtle signs such as cognitive impairment. So watch out for that one.

You might also develop depressive symptoms if your thyroid gland (an endocrine gland in your neck) is out of whack, so make sure you ask your doctor to do in-depth blood work. If you are diagnosed with hypothyroidism (underactive thyroid), it can be easily treated.

Remember, a diagnosis of depression does not reflect a character weakness or a personal failure. Indeed, depression or depressive episodes often occur in older women who have lived a normal and productive life.

If you're depressed or become depressed, what action will you take to address it?

HOW NOT TO STRESS OUT IN ONE EASY LESSON

Behind every stressful thought is the desire for things to be other than they are.

—Toni Bernhard

We can't avoid stress altogether. However, you probably have more control over the timing of stressful events than you think. For instance, if you've recently lost your husband, don't immediately sell your home. If your health is diminishing, don't panic and run off to an assisted living facility. Think things through. Delay responding if you can. Handle one circumstance at a time. Find support, get feedback, and slow down!

If predictable stressors are coming your way, try not to face them all at once. Author Sandra A. Crowe suggests, "Give yourself a break. Choose a task to postpone or delegate—cancel your dinner plans so you can enjoy a restful evening. Give yourself permission to recharge. Meditate, take a catnap, or just close your eyes and visualize comforting, enjoyable experiences."

Remember, there are enormous benefits to keeping your stress under control as you age. Our bodies are in direct communication with our emotions, and stress has an effect on all the major organs. Here are some other ways to control stress:

- Invite a grandchild or neighborhood youngster to a tea party. Being around a child can lighten your spirit and give you a new perspective.

- Get a massage. A massage can help you feel loved and nurtured. It can also ease the muscle tension and aches that sometimes accompany a bad mood.

- Petting an animal can release your stress (and your blood pressure). If you don't have a pet to stroke and care for, volunteer at the local animal shelter.

- Most important, create a loving, supportive network of friends. Not having a close friend or confidant is as detrimental to your health as smoking or carrying extra weight.

What can you do to reduce the stress in your life?

LIVING WITH LOSS

Until I can mourn the loss of a dream I cannot be comforted enough to have vision for a fresh one.

—MADELEINE L'ENGLE

As we age, we will all experience two kinds of losses: gradual and sudden. The gradual losses are things such as your eyesight not being what it used to be, your walking has become a little less stable, or, if you're like me, you're getting shorter! It's difficult for some women to accept the gradual loss of a youthful appearance. We look in the mirror and see new wrinkles or frown marks—our once familiar face now portrays a road map of our journey through life.

Sudden loss may also come in the form of a stroke, in which you might become suddenly disabled, or the death of a spouse or friend. Then there is the inevitable loss of status, sometimes gradual, sometimes sudden, as we age. Changing from wife to divorcée or widow, or from worker to retiree, is a status passage that involves a kind of death of the former self.

One way to manage loss is to gain strength and meaning from others' stories. Find a biography or autobiography or DVD of an artist, playwright, or author who has experienced loss. You may find that the negative energy of loss was turned into a creative pursuit with a positive outcome.

Going after what we have lost is a natural response, but what are we going after? Perhaps we are going after the meaning of loss in our lives. As I said in my book *I Wasn't Ready to Say Goodbye*, "Grief is not something we 'get over' or heal from as if it were an illness. It is a journey to a new stage of life. . . . The goal is reconciliation with life."

What gradual or sudden losses are you currently experiencing? Is there an opportunity for you to create meaning from the loss?

HAPPINESS, OPTIMISM, AND LONGEVITY

[The] second half of one's life is meant to be better than the first half. The first half is finding out how you do it. And the second half is enjoying it.

—FRANCES LEAR

If your emotional outlook on life is an optimistic one, you increase your chances of living longer. People who view aging as a positive experience live an average of seven and a half years longer than those who look at it negatively. Researchers at Yale say that the power of optimism is even greater than that of lower blood pressure or reduced cholesterol—each of which lengthens life by about four years.

Happy, optimistic women typically feel personal control over their lives, and those who feel they have little or no control over their lives suffer lower morale and worse health. For example, studies show that women with osteoarthritis have less pain when they're happy.

You can't blame your unhappiness simply on aging. Social scientists interviewed samples of people representing all age groups and found that no time of life is notably happier or unhappier.

How does one stay optimistic? Start by taking personal responsibility for your own happiness. Don't blame other people or external events for making you unhappy. Find what you love doing, and by all means, do it. Include things you enjoy in your life every day, even small things. Make a list of the positive events in your life, and refer to the list when you're down. Spend five minutes every day thinking or writing about what you appreciate in life. Stay focused on the positive—even bad days have at least some bright spots.

What can you do today, right now, to feel happier and more optimistic about your life?

WINTER SUNRISE

A day began with a fine winter sunrise, a long view of the distant horizon slowly taking on color. . . . In cities where I spent my young days, I was unaware of the power the sunrise could generate.

—Doris Grumbach

It's midafternoon in February, and the lack of sunshine today has me feeling down. Maybe this is a metaphor for the winter of my life. Just as the days grow shorter with the passing seasons, my life will become darker, less warm. Then I assure myself that the winter days of my life—the season of barren trees, ice on the pond, and slippery roads— only mean that life will feel more vital and purposeful, and I feel better.

Each of the seasons of my life has had its meaning and reason. The spring of my life was filled with bursts of growth, weeds and all, coupled with lots of rain (tears). The summer was languid and juicy with passion. The fall of my life (which is now) is fertile with fallen leaves and the rich compost I have created that nourishes me.

In the late fall, I will tell myself that even the fading blooms are beautiful—that even as the hydrangea begins to turn its blossoms from bright white to soft brown and lavender in preparation for winter, it is nonetheless lush with promise. I will hold the beauty of it in my eyes, bring it down into my middle to warm my bones in the winter. I'll use the fallen, dried branches I retrieve from my lawn to kindle my fire as the signs of outer, visible growing cease for the season. I know that my growth continues unseen and that there is new life in every withered branch that clings to the tree.

In your journal, write a metaphor describing the seasons of your life.

YIELDING

When two great forces collide, victory will go to the one who knows how to yield.

—Ancient Chinese philosophy

I was staying in a hotel on the beach in Puerto Rico when, from my balcony, I saw two palm trees swaying wildly in the high winds. A strong tropical storm was moving in, bending the tall trees at nearly right angles. Any other tree might have snapped under that kind of consistent, relentless force. Yet those stately palm trees were bouncing back unharmed.

The palms were yielding to the persistent force of the wind. Yielding allowed them to remain standing. And so it is with the great natural force and push of the aging process.

We need to yield to the sometimes difficult and challenging onset of our years. Pushing back hard against the inevitable force of nature is not nearly as powerful as yielding. The key is knowing when and how to yield, knowing how to push forward when necessary.

Of course, there are people and situations we just shouldn't yield to, like letting our teeth rot or living with chronic pain that could be treated. We shouldn't yield to anyone who is abusive or hurtful or to any situation that makes us feel unnecessarily diminished. You will know when it is right to yield—it will feel good. It will ultimately feel growth-producing and powerful, and the victory will be yours.

Are there some things you could choose to yield to today or that you anticipate needing to yield to in the future?

5

our fears

*Do you really want to look back on your life and see how wonder-
ful it could have been had you not been afraid to live it?*

—Caroline Myss

Suppose explorer Ponce de León really had found the fountain of eter-
nal life? Would it have made him any happier? I don't know about
him, but an AARP survey asked adults age eighteen and older if they
wanted to live to be one hundred. Guess what? Sixty-three percent of
them said no.

Despite the fact that we have a good chance of reaching one hundred (whether we like it or not), many of us fear the unknown land-
scape of aging. We fear illness, not having enough money, losing our
mental abilities, being dependent on others, and becoming a burden to
our families. Truth is, we don't have ultimate control over these situations, but we aren't completely helpless victims either. Many centenarians are still active in their communities and are practicing their skills,
enjoying their hobbies, and feeling surprisingly healthy.

My good friend Tita Buxton (age seventy-six) believes we shouldn't
focus on what we fear about aging. "By fearing the unforeseen [aging],
the future becomes what we fear." She says this can result in "a self-
fulfilling prophecy. When I read all the stuff about aging and memory

loss, I could get hung up about it rather than enjoying the life and health I do have." Tita has a point. I believe we need to face our fears and choose to live a good life in spite of them.

Remember, fear is not always bad. If you never experience it, chances are, you're living too safely. You may be living beneath your capacity and avoiding challenges. The trick is to live your life fully and to do what you have to do in spite of your fear.

FEAR OF AGING

October dresses in flame and gold
Like a woman afraid of growing old.

—ANNE MARY LAWLER

When we talk about our fear of growing old, what are we saying? Most of us are concerned and fearful of becoming disabled, weak, and sick. I'm not saying that some of that doesn't happen, but consider this: on any given day in the United States, of all our population over sixty-five, more than 80 percent, are doing just fine physically—they're fully functional and independent!

People are vigorous and healthy longer than they used to be. For example, someone eighty today may be the physical and mental equivalent of a sixty-year-old in the previous century.

I find that if I experience each passing year as an opportunity to learn something about life, I feel more positive, more alive. Author Melody Beattie writes, "Now I'm learning to welcome aging, as each decade of life brings its own challenges, joys, sorrows, and teachings. . . . I don't fear aging, for I know that it's as much, and as important, a part of my life as my youth."

My seventy-five-year-old friend Melinda Martin once told me that one of the many things no one tells you about aging is that it is such a nice change from being young. That caused me to think about some of the nice changes that have occurred in recent years. I do feel more confident and a lot wiser than I did twenty years ago. In fact, lately I've been taking exercise and diet a lot more seriously, and I'm feeling stronger. I also don't worry so much about what life will bring because at this point, I've been through a lot, both physically and emotionally, and—look!—I'm still here to write about it.

What are you most afraid of about aging, and what can you do to help alleviate your fears?

ALONE, ALIVE, AND WORRIED

Did I think more about age, aging, being and growing old when I was alone? I think so.

—DORIS GRUMBACH

Maybe you're living alone right now, or perhaps you're anticipating you will be at some time in your life. Consider that you will have a choice when the time comes. Alone is a choice, *not* a condition.

Consider this fact: People age sixty-five and over are adopting a living situation more commonly associated with students and young professionals—living with roommates to share companionship and expenses, and to provide some added security. They respect each other's independence and privacy, cook dinners for each other, help with driving, notice when the other's not feeling well, and generally provide support to one another.

Now consider these two scenarios:

1. You've been living safe and secure with your longtime husband in a three-bedroom home. Then he dies. You have some savings and a bit of income from Social Security plus a pension. When you add it all together, you have enough to maintain your home. After a year or two, your grief subsides, and you feel relatively comfortable in your home. However, each time you descend the stairs to the basement with the laundry, you worry about falling. You imagine spending a day or two with a sprained ankle just sitting

on the damp basement floor until someone realizes your predicament. If you had a roommate, she would know right away if you didn't return from the laundry room. She could call 911 for you and keep you company until help arrived.

2. You're living alone when you receive bad news by telephone concerning a dear friend. Silent and teary, you hang up the phone. Your roommate senses your despair, brings you a cup of tea, and patiently listens while you tell her what happened.

What alternate living choices are you willing to consider in the future?

FEAR OF BEING A BURDEN

I have a duty to all who care for me—not to be a problem, not to be a burden. I must carry my age lightly for all our sakes.

—FLORIDA SCOTT-MAXWELL

I ponder my own future and that of my aging women friends. Some are childless and living on their own; some have children living around the country. Who will be there for us, and do we want them to be? I'm not counting on anyone to help me with the challenges of the future, but I can't help worrying that I might someday become a burden.

Who will be there for me when I'm an old woman? Who will monitor the doctors and ask all the right questions? Who will post notes on the refrigerator reminding me of my doctor's appointment? Who will visit me? Who will help me stay engaged in the world? Who will listen to my fears and offer empathy? Who will help me set up the Christmas tree?

I felt sad recently when over coffee my sixty-eight-year-old friend Mary told me, "I'm getting to know my neighbors so that someone in my building will notice if three days' worth of newspapers are piled up outside my door!" That prompted me to think. How about we all band together? I toy with the idea of communal living, of creating an enclave of like-minded women friends sometime in the future. We could be there for each other.

The way you approach life now will affect the quality of your old age and whether or not you become burdensome. Try investing in a wider world by making friends of all ages. Make sure your doctors will be there when you need them by finding doctors who are younger than you are. Spend less and save more, pay attention to nutrition, and for goodness sake, exercise more.

We are ultimately responsible for our own lives. Even so, the time will come when we'll all need help. In my mind, when the time comes, I will not consider myself a burden. Instead I will consider that I will need, as we all do, support and encouragement from my friends and family.

What life decisions can you make now that will affect future challenges?

FEAR OF PAIN

My mother-in-law had a pain beneath her left breast. Turned out to be a trick knee.

—PHYLLIS DILLER

There are two categories of physical pain—chronic and temporary, also called acute. At different points in our lives, we will be confronted by either or both. Women tend to feel acute pain more intensely than men do. Women are also more vulnerable to a variety of painful conditions that include migraines, arthritis, fibromyalgia, pelvic pain, and abdominal pain of various kinds. Men and women both suffer back pain equally. Perhaps it's more acceptable for women to talk about their pain.

Of all symptoms, pain is probably the most upsetting, to patients as well as to doctors. But few doctors are actually trained to deal with it. Now there is a special breed of doctors called pain specialists who see pain not as incidental to disease but as a disease in its own right. Most major hospitals have a pain management team, and our choices for treating pain are wide and varied.

As you age, you are bound to run up against increased pain or discomfort from surgery, arthritis, muscle aches, and so on. If you become tense or fretful about your condition, the pain increases. The pain also increases if you are uninformed. It's a proven fact that when people prepare in advance for surgery, they have less pain and fewer complications, plus they heal faster. Preparation includes gathering honest, clear, straightforward information.

I was extremely grateful when my surgeon said I would experience acute pain after my gallbladder surgery for a period of time, that it was normal, and that it would be well managed with medication. During my overnight hospital stay, her honest words came back to me and helped me to experience less stress, in turn helping me cope with the intense discomfort.

In addition to your doctor's honest information, one of the ways to break the stress-pain cycle is to learn how to meditate. Investigate meditation classes, or buy a relevant book or relaxation CD. When it comes to surgery, for instance, start practicing the technique early so that by the time you get to the operating room, you've become a master. With practice, you will be able to lie there, elicit the relaxation response, and feel a lot better.

One of my favorite pain management techniques is visualization. I imagine I'm in one of my favorite places—the island of Kauai in Hawaii. Also known as guided imagery, this technique involves using your mind's eye to picture something that will both distract your thoughts and promote a sense of release and relaxation.

If you are fearful of pain, remember, there are ways to manage it. We need to fight, if necessary, to make our doctors listen. We are not hysterical because we cry when we are in pain. We need to demand respect and receive it, but first we need to respect ourselves, ask for what we need, and seek information about what we don't know.

Are you in physical pain? If so, what additional steps can you do to manage it?

FEAR OF LOSING CONTROL

We think . . . that we have control of our lives; we make plans, have date books and schedules, and then we turn around to see ourselves and realize our lives have their own composition, their own movement.

—Natalie Goldberg

Riding back from the library on a beautiful late March afternoon, I was met head-on at a stoplight by a speeding, out-of-control, four-wheel-drive, teenage-driven vehicle. It was just one week after I had signed the contract for my first book, titled *I Wasn't Ready to Say Goodbye.* The windows were rolled down to let in the sun and air, and the back seat was stacked with library books on death. The impact of the speeding vehicle caused me to experience extreme whiplash. I was immediately disoriented and dizzy. The police arrived within seconds, just as I was trying to call 911 on my cell phone. Amazing how difficult it is to remember those three easy numbers when your brain has banged against the inside of your skull.

One minute, I was a newly contracted, soon-to-be author; a gainfully employed psychotherapist; and a part-time consultant—the next minute, I was suffering a traumatic, closed-head brain injury. Before the accident, I had been in control of my life and the pursuit of happiness. The next day, I was dependent on others to make decisions for me, to drive for me, to think logically for me, to help me walk straight and find words, to guide me from room to room when I got lost in my own house.

I called my office and, in a halting, kindergarten voice, explained that I'd been in a car accident and that maybe it would take a week or so to recover—it ultimately took two and a half years. Most of the first year, I felt and acted like I was ninety years old or more. I had to walk with a cane so I wouldn't bang into walls. My neuropsychologist said this was normal. Not for me, it wasn't! I was a hustler, a juggler of many balls in the air. Now I was having trouble making toast and remembering the word for milk (I called it white stuff). Now I was taking a shower only to forget which comes first: shampoo or conditioner.

I'd thought I was in control of my life. I knew exactly what the plan was and where I was going. Before the accident rearranged my life, I was going to spend every Friday, all day, just working on my writing. I would see clients all day Thursdays, and after four o'clock on Mondays, Tuesdays, and Wednesdays when I got back from my consulting job. The schedule was suddenly different now, life going slower than I could have ever imagined, taking on its own composition, its own movement.

Once I could remember some words and start typing again (thank God for spell check), I found myself with endless hours to work on my book, to sit in the garden, to read for short periods, to be with my grandson and children in ways I'd never had time for in the past. When I began to give up total control of my recovery, I began to feel better. I was deepening, digging into new soil, accessing what I called my new brain, trying on another self, becoming a me I had not known before, and the control—the controller, the higher power—was driving this time.

Acknowledge that you have little control over outside events. Whatever success you enjoyed at work, whatever plans you made for the future, gave you the illusion that you had mastered the world and taken control of your own life. Brushes with death or sudden life changes can help us develop an increased awareness of how little we do control. Life goes on making its own plans, producing its own troubles and joys—and it's still worth living.

In what way has life shown you that you are not totally in control? What have you learned from those experiences?

OH NO, NOT PUBLIC TRANSPORTATION!

It's important as we age to take into account that there will be certain realities that should be faced squarely and realistically. One of these is driving.

—Tita, age 76

My husband, Steve, and I have been traveling by car to the most northerly coast of Maine for many years to a house where we spend two weeks in the fall. As we grow older, I imagine a time when we'll need to fly to Maine instead of drive, then rent a car and drive the forty-five minutes to the house where we stay. I've thought, *One day we won't be able to do even that much driving.* Am I sad about that prospect? You bet!

Driving is synonymous with independence and freedom. Never mind driving nine hundred miles to Maine—driving plays such a key role in daily life, it's no surprise that an individual's physical and mental health may suffer when driving ceases and outside activities dwindle. Transportation is the glue that holds life together. The freedom to come and go as we want, when we want, is ultimately a personal responsibility.

Health combined with age is a more important predictor of driver self-regulation than age alone. So if you're an eighty-five-year-old woman with good vision, good reaction times, and good health, keep on driving. In fact, the Insurance Institute for Highway Safety says older drivers are less likely than teenagers to hurt people in car accidents. But get your eyes checked at least once a year, and make sure your ears are working, too. You don't want to mistake honking horns for migrating geese!

I think most of us mature, evolved women are willing to self-regulate ourselves by restricting our driving under certain conditions:

bad weather, highways at night, heavy traffic, unfamiliar areas, rush hour, or long distances. Over time, it is important to develop conscious strategies to compensate for failing vision, slower reflexes, and stiffer joints. Chronic illnesses and multiple medications also make driving more challenging. Should you hang up your keys? Ask yourself these questions:

- Do I find myself saying, "Whew, that was close"?

- Do cars seem to appear from nowhere?

- At intersections, do cars proceed when I feel I have the right of way?

- Are gaps in traffic harder to judge?

- Do others honk at me?

- After driving, do I feel physically exhausted?

- Am I slower than I used to be in reacting to dangerous driving situations?

- Are family members or friends afraid to be a passenger when I drive?

- Have I had an increased number of near accidents in the past year?

When you shop for a car, look for options like automatic transmission, power brakes and steering, automatic windows, and power seat adjustments and mirrors that will help you compensate for diminished flexibility or strength. As you get older, get used to public transportation while you still drive so it won't be so hard on you later on. In planning for our futures, we need to ask ourselves the hard questions of where we would live and how we would get around if we couldn't access some form of transportation. Some rural or suburban areas have sparse public transportation and a lack of nearby goods and services. If you live in such an area, you might research privately owned shuttles, look at moving to a city, or discuss other options with family and friends.

What transportation alternatives are you willing to consider when the time comes?

FEAR OF DYING

People living deeply have no fear of death.

—Anaïs Nin

I've faced death in a real way—a head-on car crash, a near-drowning on the Salt River in Arizona, a plane that nearly plummeted to earth in a snowstorm, and a terrifying episode in 1980s civil-war-torn Mozambique where my mission executive husband and I faced a deadly ambush. I have had to confront my fear of dying.

When faced with our own mortality, we may begin to question other aspects of our lives, including the choices we have made along the way. Alongside our fear of dying, questions may arise, such as: *Did I choose the right partner? The most fulfilling career path? Am I happy with my current life, and do I have the courage to change before I no longer have options?* It's those things left undone that came to mind as I was facing death. I thought about the book I hadn't written that I had intended to write "one of these days." I was sorry that I hadn't told my husband, children, and friends often enough how much I loved them.

I'm not so much afraid of dying as I am of not having lived my life to the fullest. It's hard to use your available time with all your heart until you've eyed death on the road up ahead. These days, I'm trying hard not to put off, hold back, or save anything that would add laughter and radiance to my life and the lives of those I love. If it's worth seeing or hearing or doing, I'm doing it now so death will seem less of a punishment. Every morning when I open my eyes, I tell myself that this day is special. Every day, every minute, every breath truly is a gift from God.

And when my time comes, I will let go into an all-embracing light, as a reward, not a punishment.

What have you been putting off that you can do now?

FEAR OF ABUSE

A blessing of fear in these years is that it invites us to become the fullness of ourselves.

—Joan Chittister

About 4 percent of Americans over sixty-five are abused or neglected each year. Frequently, the abuser and abused reside together. Many are dependent on their abusers for daily care. Issues of power and control are at the core of this abuse.

No matter what age you are, domestic abuse can take on many forms. Mistreatment ranges from physical and psychological abuse to passive and active neglect. The abuse may include the exploitation of financial resources. It can also take the form of coercive behaviors such as progressive social isolation, deprivation, and intimidation; psychological, emotional, sexual, or verbal abuse of a person by a past or present intimate partner.

You need not allow someone to abuse or mistreat you just because you are older and in need of help. Some older women find themselves in situations where they need assistance with life tasks. When you feel powerless and afraid in these circumstances, you might be hesitant to bring abuse to the attention of those in a position to help. But it's very important to speak with someone who can help you. In all cases, it is essential that authorities be notified immediately—Adult Protective Services, your state's Elder Abuse Hotline, and/or victims' assistance services. Talk to your physician, clergyperson, nurse, health aide, dentist, optometrist, or other professional health care provider. These professionals recognize that they may be the only ones in a position of trust and confidence who can identify and report the abuse. Remember, your self-respect, dignity, and maybe even your life are at stake.

What action will you take if you feel abused or see someone else being abused or neglected?

FEAR OF BEING A BAG LADY

Fear is inevitable, I have to accept that, but I cannot allow it to paralyze me.

—Isabel Allende

When my friends and I get together, inevitably one of them brings up the fear of not having enough financial resources to make old age a positive experience. I respond, realistically, how much money do you need to be happy, to feel secure?

Do you think you'll be living in the street at some point in your older years? Let's look at the reality: economizing can have the effect of forcing us to think creatively about our lifestyles and our priorities, to reflect on what matters to us. Looking for ways to enjoy life while reducing the amount of money we spend builds character. It's not a disgrace.

You don't have to deplete your resources if you take action now to begin living creatively and actively seeking alternatives to spending more than you can afford. For instance, take advantage of senior discounts, offer personal services instead of giving expensive gifts, check out books and DVDs from the library instead of buying them, and discover the pleasures that can come from a walk in a beautiful place instead of shopping at the mall.

If you're worried about resources, who says you can't continue to work at a job if you want and need to? Why spend one-fifth to one-third of your life in retirement? Along with millions of other women, we are likely to be healthy and active well into our futures, so why not make some money while we're at it? Most of all, try not to live in fear. Living in fear is not really living.

In your journal, note some practical and creative ways you could economize, starting today.

FEAR OF ASKING FOR HELP

Sometimes, reaching out and taking someone's hand is the beginning of a journey. At other times, it is allowing another to take yours.

—Vera Nazarian

When I was suffering from the acute stages of a mild traumatic brain injury, I couldn't drive for almost two years. I had the reaction time, visual depth of field, and driving ability of a ninety-year-old. I needed the help of friends and family and, for the first time in my life, I had to ask for help. It was a painful lesson for militantly independent me.

Many of us have been taught that we shouldn't admit to our pain and suffering, so we bear them in silence. We begin to feel alone, yet if we need companionship, we need companionship. Let's not be fearful of asking for what we need.

Here are some suggestions: If you live alone or need help from time to time, organize a support system of friends, relatives, and organizations that you can call on. Make sure your home is organized so a helpful neighbor or friend can find what is needed to give you a hand. Make sure important names and phone numbers are handy and visible for all to see.

You'll likely appreciate others doing nice things for you, but did you know that allowing others to do things for you will also make them like you? It makes people feel good to help others. Asking someone for help is a positive, not a negative. Some things are even more fun when done with the support of someone else. Don't be afraid to ask for help.

If you had to ask someone for help, who would it be? Why?

FEAR OF THE FUTURE

You can't make decisions based on fear and the possibility of what might happen.

—Michelle Obama

Some days, I fear taking on the responsibility of planning for my future. I know I should prepare, but what if I make a mistake in the planning? Suppose I make plans for my future and then don't show up for them because I became senile instead? Suppose I forget who I made the plan for? My sister Marilyn and her husband cashed in their savings, including their IRA, bought their dream house, and he died six months later. Up and died, leaving her holding the plan.

Author Harold Bloomfield wrote, "The three most profound questions in every person's life are: Who am I? Where did I come from? Where am I going?" The root cause of human suffering, he says, is "the accumulation of unprocessed experience from the past." I think it's also the accumulation of too many hard-and-fast plans that might not come true.

I believe that women who learn to adapt, who learn to create opportunities and accept their limitations, will have a better quality of life. Women who make choices that will allow them to spend more time pursuing their passions and who have some kind of loose game plan will ultimately age more successfully.

Are you fearful of the future? If you were less fearful and more flexible, what would your life be like now?

6
our love lives and relationships

To those who have given up on love, I say, "Trust life a little bit."

—Maya Angelou

Women are finding their voice in relationships more than they ever have. Many are reassessing their long-term marriages and are challenging their mates to be more sensitive to their needs. Older women who are looking for love often find themselves struggling with issues of self-image and self-esteem.

Sharing the experience of aging with a husband, partner, or lover may not be in the cards for every woman. Even so, it's important to feel good about what makes you feel womanly. I know many older women who aren't physically attractive, but they've got joie de vivre. They have bounce; they have vitality, and that's what makes them attractive. These women don't take themselves too seriously, and they know how to laugh. They don't go around moaning and groaning about every little thing.

Most of our mothers lived restricted sex lives. Fear of expressing sexual desire helped to age our parents because of all the stipulations and anxieties on sexual freedoms. The major fears women have had are due to rules set by men on what women should and can be sexually. Even if we senior women haven't tried all the positions in the Kama

Sutra, we know we are nonetheless real women in many different areas of our lives. As we age, we need to approach our sex lives with honesty and a willingness to learn about our changing bodies. And remember, expressions of love aren't all about sex. Some women are in fulfilling relationships that are deep and abiding without it. An AARP survey revealed that 50 percent of women would choose chocolate over making love!

GET HUGGED!

> We need 4 hugs a day for survival. We need 8 hugs a day for maintenance. We need 12 hugs a day for growth.
>
> —Virginia Satir

Hugging, snuggling, petting, stroking, and touching are good for your health, your heart, and your relationships. It seems a terrible shame that such a wonderful resource is often limited to times of grief and sexual encounters. Hugging and being hugged can do a great deal to improve the quality of your everyday life. No matter your age, human touch feeds a very basic need and actually activates many biological mechanisms that help the body heal itself.

I read about a university project that trained older volunteers to massage premature, drug-exposed, or failure-to-thrive newborns. The researchers were sure the infants would experience some beneficial effects because in some earlier studies, massage therapy had resulted in decreased levels of stress and increased physical and cognitive gains for the babies. But in the study, something else happened as well: the massagers also started to benefit. They started having more social contacts and suffering less depression. Whether people are touching or being touched, they not only feel better, but they *are* better, too.

What happens if you live alone? How do you get your hugs then? When my husband traveled a great deal for his job, I turned to my cats for physical comfort. Author Eda LeShan writes, "Holding the warm body of a cat that is purring is a kind of special contact that begins to evaporate from our lives as we become widowed and children and grandchildren move far away and nobody has time for hugs." This "special contact" has clearly established medical and emotional benefits.

Find a good masseuse, and go once in a while. I ask for hugs from my grown daughter (who lives nearby) and grandson as well as several close friends. And don't forget to ask your manicurist for a shoulder massage!

Who can you ask to give you hugs each day?

EXPRESSING YOUR SEXUAL SELF

I'm intending to walk around town as a sexy old lady, the kind that no Boy Scout need hurry to help cross the street.

—Judith Viorst

Those messages from the media and society at large that an older woman shouldn't be too sexy or too vigorous or too interested in life are really upsetting. We need to fight that stereotyping. Sex is not just for the young. Baby boomer women came of age believing we had a right to sexual pleasure, and that belief is not about to evaporate.

Close ties with friends and family are as important to quality of life as sex is for some women. Of course, getting older does bring certain physical changes that can cause problems, but fortunately those can usually be treated. There are few reasons that men and women can't have active, fulfilling sex lives into their nineties. In fact, some women actually become more orgasmic in their later years.

Sexual intimacy does change as we age. For instance, around fifty, men tend to become more emotional about lovemaking, and they start seeking more closeness and intimacy. Did you know that many men have the same fears and anxieties about aging as women do and they're just as self-conscious about their potbellies as you may be about the fat on your thighs?

Women, on the other hand, become more independent and assertive. Some women don't understand that their male partners may need more foreplay and a little more understanding during sex. On the other hand, you may resent having to give more at this point in your life. If you've been harboring resentment over issues you haven't confronted as a couple, you may not be willing give more.

There are some steps you can take to feel good about yourself if you're just beginning a sexual relationship. Until you feel secure with the man you're sexually involved with, you can hide your sagging arms with sleeves. You don't have to wear a short nightgown if your knees are knobby. After a while, when you're confident in the relationship and feeling better about your older body, strut around the bedroom nude with your head held high if you want to. Self-acceptance is sexy.

Can sex get better with age? Absolutely. There's more physical pleasure, more free time, no concern about pregnancy, no children at home (usually). For couples who understand it, the slowing of sexual response can be an advantage. They tend to get more in sync.

Not everyone over fifty chooses to or can have sex. Perhaps you have a long history of lack of interest in or fear of sexual intercourse, or maybe the desire is there but there's no opportunity to meet a potential sexual partner. No matter what the cause, countless older women are living happy, contented lives without sex.

Don't be afraid to discuss issues in your sex life with your doctor or gynecologist. You may have to initiate the discussion; your doctor may not bring up this touchy subject because many medical professionals still don't think of older people as sexual beings.

In our older years, sexual desire doesn't just happen. Most women have to be physically stimulated to feel desire for their partner. Ironically, this means that women who think they need to be in the mood to have sex might in fact need to have sex to get in the mood.

The image of the older woman as sexless needs some rethinking. While sags and bulges don't necessarily symbolize sexiness in this society as well as firm young skin does, there are more intrinsic qualities that create the sexual chemistry that attracts us to each other. Sex is not just as it is portrayed in the movies. It's a lot more than that, and it's defined by our stage in life. It's an expression of our connection to our partner and to ourselves.

How do you feel about your sexual self?

WHEN HUSBANDS DIE

Staring at my ceiling,
counting dreams of you at midnight . . .

—MARILYN HOUSTON

Author Gail Godwin wrote, "It was so quiet after he was gone; there was no music, and that voice wasn't there." As I read that passage, I felt a stinging sadness. Although I deeply crave solitude and quiet, the absence of sound would be a very difficult part of losing my husband.

Grieving is the hardest work you will ever do. Even though you may spend years caring for a chronically ill husband, you may be emotionally unequipped for his death. When the final event happens, we are rarely, if ever, ready. We hope for a miracle.

Acceptance is difficult. Andrea, a client of mine, recalled the night after her husband's funeral: "I couldn't sleep, so I spent half the night cleaning the kitchen. I said the word *widow* out loud to myself, tasting its bitter sound in my mouth. Even though I'd been preparing to say this word for the two years since his leukemia was diagnosed, it was still a challenge to say it." Brenda, a sixty-one-year-old client, told me that for the first year and a half after her husband died, she couldn't concentrate enough to read a full paragraph. "I couldn't focus. When someone you love dies, a part of you dies, too. It's almost three years now, and I feel as if I am just now beginning to think."

About 50 percent of women over the age of sixty-five are widows. About 85 percent of wives outlive their husbands. Yet millions of women who no longer have husbands are doing quite well. In fact, many women do better on their own than men do. Although loss of a spouse is one of the most stressful life events one can experience, in the long term, most older women find that widowhood is accompanied by a positive shift into a new life phase. They want to take back control of their lives, test out skills they learned over a lifetime, exercise new feelings of strength and self-confidence that maturity can bring.

My friend Barbara told me, "My husband's death was, and continues to be, the most defining moment in my life. I'm the same person I was before, but now I know how strong I am." Some women begin to enjoy their single life as soon as the sharp edges of grief have worn off. Seventy-two-year-old Liz related her story. "My husband died of a heart attack. We were married for forty-one years. . . . I'm still lonely at times, but I've made some new single friends, and I'm starting to enjoy life again."

If you adopt ongoing grief as a way of life, you're still making your husband responsible for your well-being. Another danger lies in putting your deceased husband on a pedestal, which makes it easy to remember only the good so that going forward, no one else can measure up. You may be using this view as an excuse to prevent yourself from renewing your life and loving another person. The key task is to accept the reality of the death, experience the pain of grief, adjust to life without the deceased, and memorialize the loved one in order to move on.

The word *widow* comes from the Sanskrit and means "empty." But does it have to be an empty time, or can one still fill up on what life has left to offer? What are your thoughts and feelings about this?

LONG MARRIED

Love recognizes no barriers. It jumps hurdles, leaps fences, penetrates walls to arrive at a destination full of hope.

—Maya Angelou

Continued growth is possible in long-term marriage, more so than in a life dedicated solely to oneself. It is also possible to avoid finding out who you are by hiding out in the marriage and by subscribing everything to your spouse. Ask yourself, *Am I still growing in my marriage, or am I hiding out there?*

Conflicts in long-term marriages are not always what they seem. Are your conflicts actually time-of-life differences or chronic relationship patterns rearing their head anew? You may be revving up at this time in your life (children grown, nest empty, postmenopausal zest), and your husband may be winding down and readying for retirement. Developmental needs and life-cycle changes are the tectonic plates of our emotional lives. They move deep underground, outside of our control, responding to different pressures.

It's impossible to live in a long-term relationship without losing patience, without experiencing conflict, and without being thoughtless from time to time. If the love you have for your partner is strong and you have a history of practicing kindness and generosity with each other, you are more likely to prioritize those values within your relationship. You may discover you would rather be together than get your own way. This can help you move past an impasse to more loving and productive negotiations.

Think of the learning and adjusting that's already gone into your long-term marriage. As you age into retirement, you may find that you now have even more time to discover one another's gifts, explore mutual interests, enroll in courses together, or share a new sport side by side, making each other a priority.

The changes in your lives that come with age can disrupt the delicate balance of a marriage—one of you gets sick and the other now has to switch roles, or one or both of you retire and are spending a lot of time together, or the nest is finally empty—and the marriage must be redefined. Be open with your spouse about body changes, fluctuating weight, and self-image. Marriages that negotiate and navigate these physical and emotional challenges inevitably come out stronger.

I've been married to my husband for almost thirty years. We've been through challenging times, but we've managed to keep the romance alive. Here are some of my personal suggestions:

- Nurture each other's sense of humor and play.

- Write love notes to him, and leave them in unexpected places.

- Tell him you want to go out on a date.

- Send a greeting card to him at the office (or to the house if he's retired).

- Surprise him with breakfast and the sports page.

- Go with him to the doctor.

- Point out those things you appreciate about him.

- Most of all, let him know what you need. Suffering in silence never helps a marriage!

In what ways are you willing to learn and grow in your marriage?

WHEN THE ONE YOU LOVE IS ILL

After my husband's heart attack, I was coping, but then I felt overwhelmed by strong feelings of grief . . . our life together had changed forever.

—SUSAN, AGE 64

Older couples who have successfully negotiated the early stages of retirement may find themselves facing crises when illness upsets the longtime balance of roles and responsibilities in their relationship. Over the years, you developed a certain sense of security, and now the rules have changed.

Millions of older women are caring for chronically ill husbands. This stressful endeavor can be hazardous to the caregiver's health, especially in cases where the chronic disease is severe. Some caregivers begin to neglect themselves and unknowingly create stress-induced health issues.

To maintain your role as a functional caretaker, pay attention to your own needs. Take charge of your life, and don't let your loved one's illness or disability always take center stage. You're doing a very hard job, and you deserve some quality time, just for you. When someone offers to lend a hand, accept their offer. Learn as much as you can about your loved one's condition, promote your loved one's independence, grieve your losses, and allow yourself to dream new dreams.

Check with your local hospital to see if it has caregiver support groups. You will also feel less stressed if you can involve the whole family. At weekly problem-solving meetings, ask each person to describe his greatest concerns. Then discuss them. If your children are grown and living elsewhere, performing this exercise even once during a visit can break the tension and be extremely helpful.

If you are grieving over the loss of your former life with your husband, honest discussion of the changes in your relationship can ease the pain. Remember that your combined grief is both a process that may take some time and an opportunity for deepening your marriage.

How will you care for yourself should your husband or partner become ill?

DIVORCE AFTER FIFTY

*Divorce after fifty presents some problems and some special bless-
ings. . . . All of our cumulative experience gives us an advantage
in divorce. . . . You have a lot of treasure to draw from.*

—MICKI McWADE, LCSW AND LAWYER

Overall, we are a generation of women who have redefined life. Although some of us have never married, others have been married and
divorced a number of times or have been separated for so long it feels
like divorce. For some women, divorce at this stage is about the freedom that comes with liberation from a subservient role. For others,
especially those who haven't chosen it, divorce creates anxiety and fear.

Before you make the decision to divorce, be realistic. Work hard in
relationship counseling to see if the marriage is still viable. Ask yourself
if you'll be happier alone. I've had clients who left their marriages believing they would find Mr. Right, and although some did, some also
found their relationship with the new person was every bit as problematic because they didn't take the time to examine their part in the
relationship issues.

How bad does a marriage have to be before getting out is the only
answer? How much potential good remains to make it worth working
through all the problems? Let's say you've worked to resolve the problems in your relationship and have tried to accept things the way they
are. But you're still struggling with what might be best for you—stay or
leave. If you stay when you should be getting out, you risk emotional
death, and your relationship will die if you continue to obsess about
leaving.

Unfortunately, some marriages cannot and should not be saved. If
you're in a relationship with someone who is bossy, controlling, domi-
neering, overwhelming, and destructive, you may have to get out. Patterns of toxic marital interaction keep the body in a state of unhealthy
physical arousal. They create a psychological climate of helplessness

where neither spouse can surmount the hostility and negativity that has seeped into almost every marital interaction.

Contrary to popular belief, many women who need to end their marriages do quite well. Dr. Christiane Northrup, in talking about the end of her twenty-five-year marriage said, "It's a paradox that my divorce was a personal tragedy and the best thing that ever happened to me."

NOTE: If the decision to divorce is still new in your mind, remember that your spouse may find your journal and it may not be a good idea to write your thoughts or plans down where he might find them.

TRUSTING YOURSELF IN RELATIONSHIP

Trust yourself. Create the kind of self that you will be happy to live with all your life.

—GOLDA MEIR

Each year, millions of older women seek new romantic connections after divorce, widowhood, or breakups of long-term relationships, and the biggest fear is of putting trust in another partner. We don't trust our decision-making abilities. The thought of finding a new partner rekindles memories of pain, rejection, and the loss of personal identity. Perhaps you've asked yourself, *Why take the risk? Why let love ruin my life again?* This line of questioning sets us up as victims, people who are afraid to take a chance again.

Some women become less dependent on the men in their lives as they age (or evolve). Others become more dependent. Some find they've become someone they don't recognize in their relationships. They resort to behaviors that validate their partners at their own expense—they learn that to preserve their relationships, they must not be authentic, so they deny the truth of their experience.

Maybe you believe you have little to offer in a new relationship. Janet told me she has a fear of being rejected: "I'm too old, so nobody will want me." Truth is, being older is now more of a plus than a minus. There are more people over age fifty today than at any other time in history. The world is full of people your age who are looking for a person like you.

If you've lost a love relationship through death or divorce, the fear may persist that a close commitment will end in disaster. Take heart—the courage to embrace an intimate relationship will eventually overpower your fear of its possible failure or loss. As you begin to trust yourself more, you will ultimately begin to trust in others. As we grow older, every day becomes more precious. If you are alone and want to share your life with a special someone, open your heart cautiously, smile, explore with the intent to learn—enjoy and embrace life.

In what ways can you learn to trust yourself in a love relationship?

DATING AFTER FIFTY

The urge to connect with others, and to love and be loved, is ageless and universal.

—ALISON BLACKMAN DUNHAM

How does dating after fifty differ from younger years? Well, for starters, we have access to the Internet, which is a great way to sort through hundreds of interesting possibilities. The Internet is one of the best matchmakers ever for women over fifty—it's easy, inexpensive, and respectable as well as fun. It saves time, too.

One of my clients, a lovely, interesting woman of sixty-two, began dating online, and during the first year, she received over one hundred responses to her ad. Carefully following safety guidelines, she went on dates with twenty-three of the most promising prospects, and she is now engaged to a great guy.

With Internet dating, you need to follow some basic rules. Be truthful but stay anonymous for as long as you feel okay doing so, regardless of your potential date's questions. Be less concerned for his feelings than for your own safety. If he refuses to give you his work and home numbers—if he won't say what he does (or did) for a living but insists on knowing where you live or work—end the conversation. If he tells you a sad story and asks for money, run! Does hitting the delete key seem rude to you? With online dating, this is totally acceptable.

If you decide to meet him, use common sense and choose a busy public place for safety reasons. Keep the meeting short, about one hour for the first date. Take yourself to and from the meeting place on your own. Let someone know where you're going and when you'll be back.

Older women struggle with redefining themselves because the last time they were single was probably in their twenties. If there's any one rule to adhere to, it's this: be yourself and maintain an active interest in the world around you. Anyone can be desirable—first you need to believe you are. The mature men I interviewed for this book said that in general, the woman they find most attractive is the woman who knows who she is, who has a sense of playfulness and vitality, and who doesn't neglect her health. This leads to the question, if you have chronic health issues or a disability, are you less attractive? They told me not necessarily—it's the woman's attitude that's important.

What attributes do you bring to the dating table?

CHOOSING COMMITMENT AFTER FIFTY

The second time around has been not so much about correcting past mistakes as about the willingness to make new ones.

—Ana Veciana-Suarez

Some older women are choosing to get married again or live together in committed relationships, and they find these relationships peaceful, gratifying, liberating, and rich in companionship. These women typically are free from the pressures of working and raising families, and due to their added years of life experience, they are often highly aware of what they're looking for in a mate.

Life isn't all roses, however. Difficulties may come up if adult children are concerned that a new spouse will usurp their role in decisions regarding care should their parent become sick. Or they may be worried about losing their inheritance. Despite the potential stumbling blocks, many people in late-life marriages say they have never been happier.

More than 200,000 women over fifty are headed for the altar; for most of them, it's the second time around. For some of them, it's actually the first time. A friend recently told me the story of a fifty-one-year-old family member who married for the first time because it took her that long to find the right guy. We're even coming up with new definitions to describe these late-life marriages. *The Dictionary of the Future* gives this definition: "Elderweds: People age 60 or older who are marrying for the first time or remarrying."

Serious relationships in later life are a bit more complicated financially than for younger couples, and it's important to consult with a financial advisor or an attorney or both. There may be family members to care for, such as children from a prior marriage, ex-spouses, and parents. The couple may have heavy financial obligations or debts, alimony payments, or child support. They may have piled-up assets in which others have a stake. Financial advisors say you might consider a prenuptial agreement if either of you owns a business or has children. Then plan to change your will after getting married so you can update beneficiary designations on retirement plans and insurance policies.

Creating a successful marriage can be the most difficult challenge of an adult's life. At the same time, few accomplishments are more important to happiness, health, fulfillment, and satisfaction in life than a healthy, committed relationship.

If you were in the position to make a new commitment to either marriage or living together, would you?

7
our spiritual self

*The spiritual path . . . is simply the journey of living our lives.
Everyone is on a spiritual path; most people just don't know it.*

—Marianne Williamson

The spiritual journey is a lifelong process of discovery. One of our most important tasks as women is to find what spiritual truths and principles work best for us as we live out our lives. The outcome of this endeavor is not necessarily to find which religion you should join or which faith you should switch to. The community of like-minded seekers or believers is essential for some, and for others, this search has more to do with a private connection to the universe or an internal divinity.

In my practice, I've seen women express a deep, previously unspoken desperation to connect with the spiritual self. They find there is a void in their lives and that aging is a much more challenging experience because of this void.

I didn't think as much about my spiritual life previously as I do now. For many years, I was too busy making a living, raising a family, and having all the anxieties that go along with those earlier years. Now my spiritual attitude colors everything I do, everything I think, everything I read. The values and goals that served me well in the first half of my life have become less relevant as family, career, and health considerations have shifted and changed.

Whether we reach up for God, look out into the world for the goddess, or seek a divine spark within, we need to honor and value our personal search, understanding that the attributes of aging facilitate and enhance this search. Through a lens of perception that views and reflects back the world in a unique way for each of us, we consider the role of spirituality in our lives with varying degrees of intensity and involvement. At each phase of our continuing evolution, some spiritual truths will work better for us than others.

Our spiritual self is an essential aspect of ourselves—you may call it the higher self, the real self, the center, or the God within. It feels like home when we connect with it. Psychoanalyst Carl Jung used the simple, capitalized word *Self* to indicate that this place within us is connected to that which is greater than our individual and conscious identity.

You can face whatever is associated with aging with added strength and humor if you take your spiritual journey seriously. Recognize that your life is joined to others and to something greater than yourself, and you will have a compelling personal grace and naturalness that is unaffected by your passing years.

SPIRITUALITY AND HEALTH

Spirituality for me is recognizing that I am connected to the energy of all creation.

—OPRAH WINFREY

As women in this country enjoy longer lives and better health than previous generations, and as the population inches toward being more senior than junior, we are becoming as interested in the effects of aging on the human spirit as on the human body.

A study confirmed that people who go to church, synagogue, or mosque regularly tend to have lower blood pressure, stronger immune systems, and lower rates of cancer, heart disease, and mental illness—they live longer as a result. The researchers found that the life expectancy gap between those who attend more than once a week and those who never attend is over seven years. Another study showed that spiritual beliefs are more important for good health than not smoking!

People who pray or meditate experience the relaxation response—a drop in blood pressure, heart rate, and levels of stress hormones such as cortisol. Even if you do not pray or meditate, having religious or spiritual beliefs can reduce anxiety.

While factors that often accompany religious activity, such as strong social ties and healthier lifestyles, play a role in lengthening life, there is something more going on. One theory is that the social support from spiritual communities such as churches, meditation groups, or yoga classes helps people buffer the harmful effects of stress. Not all spiritual beliefs are equally beneficial. People with positive spiritual beliefs, such as the idea that God represents love and forgiveness, do better than those who believe in harsh divine punishment.

Suppose attending a religious service isn't for you. You can still feel spiritual by setting aside twenty minutes daily for quiet time—meditating, listening to music, or simply thinking about the wonders of nature or a memorable line from a poem. Read inspirational books, poetry, or essays. Read the works of philosophers or theologians. Be part of a small spiritual community that gives to others.

Is it time to take your spiritual growth more seriously? Would it help to attend a regular religious service or to do something else?

SPIRIT IN THE SILENCE

I know the gifts of Spirit not only when I hear the rippling of tongues but also in the gift of silence, when understanding and joy come without words.

—MADELEINE L'ENGLE

As I write this, I'm at a friend's beach house on Plum Island, Massachusetts, where the silence is palpable. I don't often realize how much I miss the silence until I'm immersed in it, as I am this morning. I hear the tranquilizing hymn of the waves baptizing the shoreline. I feel the reverence of the pulsing sunrise peeking over the horizon, the litany of the ocean's expanse, the laughing liturgy of seagulls. My age does not matter in these sacramental moments of connection with spirit.

In the silence, I feel my life's pulse. I wait. I listen. I understand that I am in a spiritual realm that I did not create. I understand that I am luxuriously immersed in my choice to be in solitude and to be in the fullness of my own presence.

I promise myself that this will be a priceless gift I give to myself daily. Each day, I will carve out of chaos a silence where I listen for spirit to rise in me, noiseless as a sunrise on Plum Island.

As Sue Bender wrote, "If we never pause long enough to get to know the silence, how will we know what possibilities it contains?"

Find time for solitude and silence. Then write about your experience of it in your journal.

OBITUARIES AND INSPIRATION

Fall was coming. . . . Sadie still held her vigil in the window, but now a shawl was curled about her shoulders to ward off the chill.

—SARAH L. DELANY

I enjoy reading the obituaries of women who have lived long into their lives. Here are some of my favorites from *The New York Times*:

Sophie, 96: "A leading Orthodox Christian educator whose life encompassed the history of twentieth-century Russia and the experience of Russian émigrés, died in Valley Cottage, New York, on Friday. Author of many books, at 77 Sophie wrote her memoir *Many Worlds: A Russian Life.* At the time of her death she was working as president of Religious Books for Russia, and she continued traveling and lecturing into her nineties."

Evelyn, 90: "Beloved wife. . . . Loving mother and grandmother. . . . Former Executive Secretary. . . . As a Gray Lady during WWII she comforted the troops when they returned from battle."

Sylvia, 89: "Beloved wife of the late Samuel, formerly of New York City. Loving mother of Eleanor and Bill. Dear sister of Mildred and Leon. Loving grandmother of Deborah, Will, Sarah, and Rebecca. Caring great aunt of Jeff."

Lorraine, 97: "Died peacefully at home in the arms of her beloved husband of 53 wonderful years. . . . Loving mother . . . adored niece . . . devoted friend to many. Lorraine, an effervescent woman of great charm, intelligence, courage, spirit, understanding, compassion, wit, and humor, had the marvelous gift to make people laugh and feel alive. Lorraine will be deeply missed by all."

I wonder how my obituary will read. Will I be remembered as beloved, loving, and caring of someone? As one "whose life encompassed" . . . what? Maybe I'll write my own obituary, store it with my will with strict instructions to use it word for word. "She lived, she died, and in between she tried to make a difference in the world." No. Maybe I shouldn't be selfish. Let them (whoever's left) write it up. It will probably help them grieve. Hopefully they knew who I was. Hopefully, I knew who I was.

Unless you're totally unself-conscious, you hit a stage about age fifty when you start to realize that you're not going to be here forever.

The message that no matter what you do, you'll die anyway is neither depressing nor hopeless. It's a challenge, an invitation to come back to something more meaningful in your life than an impossible attempt to recapture youth.

What would you like your obituary to say about you?

JOURNALING THE DAYS

Another reason for writing in your diary is to discover that the ideas in you are an inexhaustible fountain.

—BRENDA UELAND

Author Annie Dillard once said, "How we spend our days is how we spend our lives." Inspired by this quote, I've decided to be more intentional in my journaling, to explore just how I'm spending my days. Like currency, am I spending too much on the minutiae or the irrelevant? Am I spending well past my limit? Creating too much metaphorical debt and not reimbursing myself? Every so often, I hear someone say, "I just don't know where today went!" I'm reminded that the days are numbered—just so many left in the account.

Journaling is a way to keep track of how we spend our days. It can be a spiritual or personal balance sheet. Tuesday, I spent too much time in contemplation and not enough time getting work done. On Thursday, I spent too much time getting the mundane done and not enough time in reflection. Journaling has taught me the fine art of balance, and the discipline has helped me become more aware of who I am, what my passions are, and how I relate to spirit.

Consider keeping two journals—one for everyday contemplation and reporting and another titled "Things I Love," starting each line or paragraph with the words *I love . . .* My first entry says, *I love writing with a fountain pen.* My second entry says, *I love the way my adult son kisses me on the forehead.* Another says, *I love the first buds of spring on the maple trees in my yard.* Glue in pictures from magazines or photos you love. Whichever method you choose, a journal will help you explore who you are by identifying what you love and how you spend your days.

How are you spending the currency of your days?

INTUITION AND WISDOM

We all have an inner voice, our personal whisper from the universe. All we have to do is listen.

—C. J. HECK

To move successfully through the first years of adulthood, many women were encouraged (or forced) to view the world as a rational, competitive, hierarchical, patriarchal, and materialistic place. Fortunately, now that you're in the second half of your life, you can abandon that limiting view of the world. Hopefully now you're ready to ask deeper questions and to learn to listen to your inner voice.

I believe with all my heart that a woman's innate intuition sharpens and her wisdom deepens as she evolves and becomes older. If you listen carefully, your inner wisdom will guide you in ways to care for your aging body, your mind, and your spirit. No more discounting what you know is true about your world and yourself! When you feel an intuitive pull to call a friend or relative, follow through. When you feel a certain decision isn't for your highest good, change your mind. If you're asked to do something or go somewhere that doesn't feel right in your gut, refuse to do it.

Now is the time to fully own your intuitive wisdom and power.

Write about an intuition you had regarding a situation and what you did about it.

FINDING PEACE

What, then, is "spirituality," defined not in the usual way but as it pertains to the woman wanting to find peace with the universe? It is a feeling that the world is basically beautiful and filled with wonder, that there is a dimension of life beyond what is known.

—MARY MCCONNELL

At sixty-five, Selma's life goal was to experience something she had rarely known—peace, plain and simple. She had endured forty-five years in an emotionally abusive marriage, and it needed to end if she was ever going to experience peace. I don't think we necessarily need to make as drastic a life change as divorce to find peace. Yet finding peace does require a change of attitude and a willingness to be proactive in the search for it.

Jane, fifty-seven, is the mother of two teenagers. She's seeking peace also—the kind of peace that comes with solitude and time for herself. Her tonic is the arts. She finds a peace there that is helping her navigate the stresses of motherhood and aging. "It's hard to stay in an unsettled place when gazing at a magnificent painting or listening to music I love," she told me. "Even taking a half hour or so to fool around with paints or play the piano diverts my attention to a more centered place."

As mothers, we may have put off finding great chunks of peace and solitude until the children were grown and gone. For author Lynne Zielinski, peace comes in the form of the little things. She writes, "I am so grateful for the gifts of my autumn—opportunities to experience simple pleasures that, in times past, scurried by unnoticed in the maelstrom of raising children."

I find peace in being close to nature. No matter how I feel, the sun still rises and sets each day. Sitting in my garden, strolling on a beach, or lying on a hillside and gazing at the sky gives me a sense of peace and a connection to something greater than myself.

How can you create some peace in your life?

Getting Older Better

CHOOSING TO BE AUTHENTIC

The choices we make determine who we become, offering us the possibility of leading an authentic life.

—Jean Shinoda Bolen

Some of my most memorable, life-giving moments were connected to my younger years performing in the professional theater. However, at a certain point, I needed more predictable income that caused me to work a job I wasn't meant to be doing. For most of us when we were younger, work formed the structure of our time, and most of our activities were organized from outside ourselves rather than from within. We settled for unchallenging jobs that provided a paycheck and seemed benign enough, except that we weren't expressing our authentic selves one tiny bit.

Why do we keep some of our gifts a secret? What we have difficulty acknowledging is usually the very thing we need to confront and resolve. When we deny parts of ourselves, we are limiting the options we have in life—we are not living the life that spirit intended. The great irony about hiding our gifts is that we think it will simplify our lives. However, hiding takes tremendous energy you could be spending in other more fulfilling areas of your life. Stop putting up with situations you hate, and stop making excuses to yourself and anyone else who'll listen, while ignoring the persistent need to live authentically.

Fortunately, when you finally let yourself be authentic, the sky does not fall. I know from embracing my own authenticity that there is a queasiness at first, followed by a lightness and a sense that you are in the right place. Things begin to unfold, passions are expressed, and miracles happen.

You may wonder, *Will the world love me if they know who I really am?* The answer is: not everyone and possibly everyone. The deeper you dig within yourself and the more you expose, the more you connect with the rest of the world. You end up finding out a shocking and beautiful truth: there are people out there who really do want to hear what you have to say and who love you even more because you are fully who you were meant to be.

If you embraced and expressed your authentic, spirit-filled self, how would your life be different?

ARE YOU A GODDESS?

The Goddess does not rule the world. She is the world. Manifest in each of us.

—STARHAWK

My older sister Marilyn and I began to play with the idea that all women are goddesses after age fifty—that is, we are powerful and beautiful and come in all different sizes and shapes. Just in case you're interested in discerning whether or not you qualify as a goddess, we decided to have fun putting together the following lists.

Goddesses wear (if they want to):

- Beautiful, silky caftans or muumuus

- Earrings that swing and make soft tinkling sounds

- Sequins in the daytime

- Long skirts with slits

- Colored eye shadow

- Comfortable, supportive, attractive shoes that don't hurt

- Clothes that feel creamy, soft, and nurturing

- Cashmere, fleece, and velvet whenever they want to

- Beautiful bras and sexy panties to bed under their sleepwear (especially if they are sharing their bed with a lover)

- Whatever colors make them feel good, happy, and alive

- More than one ring on each hand

Goddesses never wear:

- Tight waistbands or tight anything

- What the designers tell them to

- High, spiky heels that hurt

- Spandex

- Double-knit polyester anything

- Days-of-the-week underwear

- Big hair or headbands

- Cinch belts

Goddesses can have:

- Fifteen flavors of tea in the house

- Chocolate anywhere, anytime

- Lip gloss in the pocket of every coat and jacket

- Christmas lights up all year long in the bedroom, kitchen, or living room

- Gingersnaps for breakfast

- Picnics in bed

- As many lovers as they want

- Wind chimes hanging everywhere

- A good belly laugh whenever they want

- Pink 25-watt bulbs in every lamp in the house

- 150-watt bulbs for reading erotic poetry

- As many candles, incense, and bags of potpourri as they can afford

Goddesses must:

- Be outrageous

- Have their own laptop

- Get a facial once a year and a pedicure at least once a month

- Save up for a girls' weekend away

- Remember that round is a shape

- Flirt all they want, especially with younger men

We are all the Goddess in many guises and forms. Marianne Williamson says, "What mature women want is this: the lightheartedness of our youth with the added depth our suffering of the past few years has given us. Through the grace of the Goddess, it is within our grasp to have both." I, for one, believe her.

In what ways can you embrace your goddess-self?

LIBERATION FROM MATERIAL THINGS

Happiness is not about collecting material things. . . . It's about having a deep feeling of contentment and knowing that life is a blessing.

—JEIGH ILANO

Sometimes it feels as if my possessions own me. I feel them saying: "Wash me, dust me, read me, polish me, pack me away for the winter, move me, unpack me for the summer, listen to me!" How can we get to any kind of spiritual illumination or growth when we're so darn busy taking care of houses, attics, basements, and storage bins full of the detritus of the first fifty years of our lives?

In school, I studied with an eighty-year-old rabbi who came into class and announced, "I've given away all the books in my library." I was stunned. What is a rabbi (or any religious professional, for that matter) without a library? When the class asked why, he replied, "Because my books were all talking to me at the same time!" I think of him every time I look around my house and hear the sounds of my possessions.

Many of my older female friends feel that if a large enough number of us went through a cultural shift from the material path to a more spiritual one, it would be of great benefit to us all.

What possessions of yours are making the most metaphorical noise?

8

our creative self

The most insidious and common manifestation of repressed creativity in women is depression.

—C. DIANE EALY

My mother was part of a generation of women who dedicated their lives to their husbands and kids in the 1940s and 1950s and never got to fully find out who they were as creative beings. I feel sad about that.

The older woman is more than just a physical body, a brain, or a social unit; she also carries within her a remarkable, authentic, hidden self that can contribute greatly to the creative process. Dancer and choreographer Martha Graham said it best: "There is a vitality, a life force, a quickening that is translated through you into action, and because there is only one of you in all time, this expression is unique."

Just as too much sustained stress is harmful to your health, sustained attention to something you really love and find fulfilling has the converse effect. Creative activity can even help us climb out of the pit of depression. In addition, research shows that creativity has a direct impact on health and longevity. For example, in patients with rheumatoid arthritis who wrote about stressful life experiences, writing significantly reduced the severity of their arthritis.

For a variety of reasons, many women don't discover their potential until they grow older. One reason is that many women are too busy working and raising families to seriously pursue creative arts. Time, which has been viewed as the enemy of the old, is actually more plentiful later in life. Rather than old age being a time of constriction, it can be a time of serious expansion and liberation.

A growing number of older women are delving into some kind of artistic expression, and they're finding that being creative is very invigorating and challenging. They discover their uniqueness and begin to get a much larger vision of what gives meaning and value to their lives.

Older artists have more confidence and courage and are often willing to take greater risks than younger ones. A young woman of twenty-one might say, "I'm not going to do that. I'll look like an idiot for trying." Whereas a sixty-five-year-old woman might say, "I'm going to give that a try—what've I got to lose?"

When you make art as an older woman, you're immersing yourself in history, memory, stories, and relationships. This is an opportunity to place yourself in your own life. You don't necessarily need to have any training—you simply need to be open to revelation and to have a willingness to express it.

IT'S NEVER TOO LATE TO CREATE!

Every arrangement of flowers made, every castle sculpted in sand, or closet reorganized touches upon our creative potential.

—Barbara Diane Barry

How many times have you said to yourself, *I wish I had . . .* or *I wish I could . . .* ? Well, is it too late? If blind painters can paint, if the hearing impaired can write and perform music, if the crippled can choreograph a dance, what's to keep you from being creative? Your age?

At the age of 104, retired teacher Sarah L. Delany collaborated with her sister, Dr. Bessie Delany (then 102), to write the *New York Times* bestseller *Having Our Say: The Delany Sisters' First 100 Years.* Their book was adapted to the stage and became a Broadway hit, and at 105 and 103 years of age, the Delany sisters published a sequel! You think you're too old?

We can create out of seeing the world through our individual and unique lifelong experiences. We've seen so much more of the world at our age, so we bring even more juice, wisdom, and fire to whatever it is we create at this time in our lives.

Here are some other women to inspire you:

- Grandma Moses was still busy painting at one hundred.

- Jessica Tandy won an Oscar at age eighty-one.

- Imogen Cunningham, an accomplished American photographer, was still teaching at the Art Institute of San Francisco in her nineties.

- Hilda Doolittle, poet and writer, wrote *Helen in Egypt,* considered one of her strongest works, at the age of seventy-five.

These women didn't allow themselves to fold up, sit in a chair, and wait for Meals on Wheels. And if you are waiting for your meal to arrive, you can still create while you wait.

What creative project can you start today?

CLAIMING THE CREATIVE SELF

I'm a singer who wants to be a writer, and a writer who wants to grow up to be an artist. I don't want to do anything in the same way I did it before.

—Letty Cottin Pogrebin

Singer Joni Mitchell, who became an artist later in life, mentioned a report card in which her sixth-grade teacher noted, "Joan should pay attention to other subjects than art." More than half a century later,

Joni Mitchell went back to her hometown with five hundred of her paintings, drawings, and photographs, and eighty-seven of Joni's works were chosen for a show in the public gallery there!

Her teacher's unkind remark touched on something in me long forgotten: how people, early in my life, affected my dreams and career decisions. When I mentioned my desire to be an actress at age fifteen, my parents said I'd be better off getting a "real job." Later in life, when I confessed that I wanted to be a writer, they reminded me how many writers were starving (wish they could see me now!).

So is it too late to begin reclaiming the creative woman within you? Think back to what was said to the younger you—rail against the negative dictates—become militant. Get angry and go paint. Paint anger. Paint the face of the person who told you that you couldn't paint; then go sell their portrait in your hometown gallery!

Melody Beattie in *Journey to the Heart* writes, "Who told you you weren't creative? Stand tall, speak up, and tell them they're wrong. . . . Allow your creativity to heal and flourish." Go to the karaoke bar and sing. Dance like Isadora Duncan in your bare feet, color outside the lines, and break the rules.

How can you reclaim and express your creative self?

CREATIVITY AND HEALTH

Since I was 60 I've written more and had better energy and more energy than I ever had in my life.

—MERIDEL LE SUEUR

Expressing the natural, vibrant force that is our creativity can improve our health, both physically and mentally. Creativity boosts our mood and increases our morale. Creativity strengthens the connections between brain cells and assists our memory. It offers a fresh way to respond to problems and may allow us to transcend them.

Living a creative life can make it easier to face adversity, such as the loss of a spouse or serious illness. With a fresh perspective, our emotions become more resilient. Capitalizing on creativity promotes a positive sense of well-being that can boost the immune system, helping us to fight disease.

Stuck creative energy can equal poor health. A colleague of mine kept putting off her desire to sing and developed a health issue that showed up around the throat area. A client with cancer told me of her desire to create her own line of jewelry, and when she did, her sore back began to heal. I suffered headaches for years before I realized that the stuck energy in my head had to become a book!

During the second half of life, women who devoted their lives to their families, and some who worked outside the home, can revisit long-postponed passions. Creativity requires an acceptance of your uniqueness and of being imperfect. With the wisdom that comes with maturity, we know ourselves better, and we learn that making a mistake won't destroy our self-image or the opinions others have of us. So get creative! It can even make you healthier.

Have you identified stuck energy in your creative life? What would you like to do about it?

DANCING FROM A WHEELCHAIR

For many older artists, that playful, free spirit helps them to find solutions to the problems of their changing abilities.

—ALEXANDRA STODDARD

The simple definition of creativity is to bring into existence something new and valued—a symphony or life-changing invention. However, what you bring into existence can also be a recipe, a well-planned vegetable garden, or a timesaving new route to a friend's house. Gene Cohen, MD, said, "As the lead researcher of a 25-year study on creativity . . . in more than 200 senior citizens, I learned that anyone can be creative." Despite those findings, some of us think we're too old and uninspired to create.

Consider Katherine Dunham was a star of countless international dance tours as well as Broadway and Hollywood musicals from the 1940s on. At ninety-one, even though she was wheelchair bound at the time, Dunham continued to lead a busy life teaching dance classes!

Perhaps life is too busy for you to slow down enough to find your creative spirit. Author Susan K. Perry, PhD, writes about a seventy-one-year-old woman who "knew she'd write her life story someday. But her real life kept getting in the way. She sold real estate and bred show horses, married four times and raised three daughters." Now that the children are grown and she's retired from real estate, she's writing short stories and a memoir. Susan reports that she's having a blast.

What obstacles to your creativity can you overcome?

PUT IT ON PAPER!

Whatever coaxes us out of hiding, to write, record, and express, is a revolutionary act. It says that we believe our lives count.

—SARK

If you want to write a poem, write a poem. Write a journal; write an epic or a screenplay. Don't worry about who will see it. If someday you decide to share it, then share it. Write whatever you write for just yourself. Write for no particular reason, or do it for a way to explore your feelings. Anne Morrow Lindbergh once wrote, "I began these pages for myself, in order to think out my own particular pattern of living, my own individual balance of life, work, and human relationships." Anaïs Nin wrote many journals from the time she was sixty-three to the time of her death at age seventy-four. Her journals provide us with a candid, passionate account of her voyage of self-discovery.

Once you start putting it (whatever it is) on paper, be kind to yourself. Even published writers have been known to judge themselves, and they shouldn't. Sue Bender, best-selling author of two of my favorite books, said, "I've written two books using struggle as my method. But after seventeen years of this single-minded obsession with writing, I still didn't think of myself as a writer." Interesting, huh?

Perhaps setting your mind on writing will give you motivation for life. At 107, author Sarah L. Delany said, "I'm going to get to work on another book! . . . It's not ambition that drives me. It's having a sense of purpose. A reason to get up every morning."

Begin, and then begin again. Put it on paper, scrap paper, unlined craft paper, loose-leaf paper, fine linen writing paper, paper napkins, small spiral notebooks with angels on the cover, newsprint, emails to yourself, large journals, desk blotters, book margins with pencil. Discover your unique self—reveal your soul.

Use your journal to put something on paper (such as an idea for a poem, a book, or an essay).

CREATIVITY AND LONGEVITY

There is a fountain of youth . . . the creativity you bring to your life. . . . When you learn to tap this source, you will truly have defeated age.

—SOPHIA LOREN

Blood pumps when we do something creative—vessels open in the brain, and circulation renews the spirit. If you're stuck thinking creativity is only smearing paint on canvas, writing a novel, or chipping a sculpture out of marble, then your creative spark might end up stuck forever. Isn't planting a garden an act of creativity? Writing a letter to a friend? Isn't setting the table with a pretty pattern or bright colors an act of creativity every bit as remarkable as oil paint on canvas? Aren't a beautifully made bed, an artfully arranged bookshelf, or a collection of candle holders all valuable as artwork?

We manifest health if we are willing to see the way we live as a creative expression. Even the small, tedious chores can be seen this way. Vacuum the carpet, and notice the lines and swirls the vacuum makes. Dust the furniture, but make a doodle in the dust before you wipe it away. Hang clothes to dry, watching as they flap about in the breeze against a blue sky.

Everywhere your eyes land, there is a palette of color, a myriad of textures, and an opportunity to live creatively. You are living a creative life if you view your world through a different lens every day, like seeing the rainbows in the soap bubbles as you wash the frying pan.

What can you do to live life more creatively?

WRITE A BOOK?!

Sometimes I believe these books are already written and my job is simply to allow them to come through me. My job is to get out of my own way.

—SUE GRAFTON

How many times have you said to yourself, *If I only had the time I'd . . . ?* Fill in the blank. Maybe you filled in that blank with, *I'd write a novel,* or *I'd write my memoirs, or I'd keep a journal.* So what are you waiting for? Isn't it time to start if you haven't already? If you've started a book, what's keeping you from finishing it? How many blank journals do you have that you've never written in because you think someone might find them when you're dead? So what?

Don't think you have the time? Julia Cameron, screenwriter and author advises, "If you are interested in writing a book, write for a few minutes every day. . . . After a few weeks you'll be encouraged by how much you have accomplished." Author Frances Weaver says, "Until we reached this wondrous age, we had not enough time of our own to sit down in a quiet place, collect our thoughts, let our imagination and memory float free, and enjoy our own heads. Now we can do that, and we write." Think you've got nothing relevant to say at your age? You're wrong.

Don't think you can get published? Then find out about self-publishing. Investigate an electronic publisher. Or do as an older woman I know who writes poetry. She prints out copies from her computer, staples them together, and gives them as gifts. These days, there's just no excuse for not getting your written work out there.

What can you start writing about today? What would the title of your book be?

9
our health

Of all the self-fulfilling prophecies in our culture, the assumption that aging means decline and poor health is probably the deadliest.

—MARILYN FERGUSON

Our tendency in this country is to treat old age like a problem desperately in need of a remedy. However, fewer Americans are becoming chronically disabled as they age. The odds of staying independent into old age and of staying out of a nursing home have been getting better with each passing year. What's behind the trend? Experts say there are a number of factors at work, among them: increasing education, improvements in maternal nutrition and public health, fewer people smoking, new drugs for heart disease and hypertension, healthier lifestyles, and advances in medical technology.

Obviously, getting old is mainly a matter of avoiding illness, and genes have a lot to do with that. But so does our behavior. According to researchers, making a big deal out of small troubles and slothful physical habits can reduce our genetic life expectancy by about ten years.

Today's healthy seventy-year-old women are doing what fifty-year-olds did a generation ago. It's not necessarily about how we live but about how well we're able to live. More than half of baby boomers will live past eighty-five, and we've got to make smart decisions about our health.

CONSIDER THE SOURCE

I am being hit from all sides with things I must do, foods I must eat, ways I must think to stay forever young. I get exhausted just thinking about it.

—Hila Colman

Author Susan Calvert Finn, PhD, says that when we evaluate health information, we should consider the source. She suggests, "Check who funded the research if results benefit a particular food or drug. Also consider the study subjects. Animal research may not apply to people, and research on men or women may not apply to the other sex." She says we should look for multiple studies on the same topic.

Consider the source—look for multiple studies on the same topic. Many of us don't have the time for research at the library or on the Internet (and whom do you believe there?) to access multiple studies on the use of yogurt spread versus the spread made with soy milk. Is jelly that's made from organically grown red currants better for me than Smuckers? I just want to eat my toast in peace. Whom do we believe? What about my cholesterol? What about my liver? Fiber, fat, sugar, phytoestrogens, nutritional supplements, herbs, high blood pressure meds. Whom do we trust? One day, I'm supposed to be eating one thing, drinking another. The next day, the news report says I have it backwards—or does it? Consider the source.

Yesterday I tripped and nearly fell trying to find my glasses so I could read the nutritional information on the cereal box. I quickly became agitated, and when I become agitated, that gets in the way of my feeling peaceful, and constant agitation is bad for your health (so is falling down). I'm caught in the sticky web of multiple nutritional studies and funded research. I'm getting a migraine from surfing the National

Institutes of Health website. Maybe the radiation from the computer screen is a health hazard. Maybe looking up websites on what's healthy is unhealthy for me.

I'll pay attention to the studies, but I'm also going to start paying attention to my body and the intuition I've been given. I reside in a wise, finely tuned instrument that knows (if I listen) when I'm abusing it, and it lets me know.

How would your life be if you listened more carefully to your body?

YOGA AND YOGURT

I tried doing just yoga and eating yogurt to lose weight and I felt like a starving pretzel.

—MARY ALICE

I've been attracted to yoga in the past few years, mainly because the only gear you need is a towel, loose-fitting clothing, and clean socks without holes. And I had read that the Delany sisters, who lived to be well over one hundred, did some yoga stretches every day.

So one day I found myself sitting cross-legged on the orange-carpeted floor of a yoga center in my town. I was feeling optimistic and nervous. Although this was a beginning yoga class, the students around me exuded a confidence in their bodies I knew I wanted to have. I started out feeling as meditative as a buddha, and when I glanced in the mirror, I saw I actually looked like one! Belly protruding, look of serenity on my face. I watched as one of the younger women in her forties lay down on the floor and brought her legs over her head. Buddha or not, I was not attempting that one!

What is yoga? The word itself is derived from the word *yoke* in Sanskrit. It's a mind-body discipline that was developed in India some five thousand years ago. Hatha yoga is a series of slow, deliberate poses that enhances flexibility, improves circulation, and increases concentration.

Pleasure is the real reason I practice yoga. The need for exercise and flexibility got me to sign up for the class. But I returned again and again for something else. During the class, the ego disappears—the me who measures her body against all the other women, the me who worries about her credit card debt. My ego evaporates, and what is left? It's hard to explain, but it feels like my truest self.

What are you willing to do to help your body feel peaceful and flexible?

FOOD IS MY FRIEND

I've never had any problem with cholesterol. As we say at the American Institute of Wine and Food, "Small helpings, no seconds. A little bit of everything. No snacking. And have a good time."

—Julia Child

You don't need me to tell you that regardless of how much you weigh, your metabolism has likely slowed down. Simply put, if you don't modify your eating habits to accommodate this change in metabolism, you'll gain weight.

Grandma always said, "You are what you eat." She lived to be 102 eating steak cooked in butter, baked potatoes with sour cream, and rice pudding with fresh whipped cream. I read in the *Worcester Telegram & Gazette* that Mary Marques, age 104, attributed her longevity to eating lots of vegetables and drinking a glass of red wine every day.

Before I turned fifty, I ate apple pie for breakfast, fettuccini alfredo for lunch, mashed potatoes and gravy for dinner, and tiramisu for dessert—who would want to change that menu?! But the pounds were packing on faster than I could count them. I want to reduce my risk of heart disease, so now I eat two to three servings of whole grains a day. I eat a cup of oatmeal for breakfast and a sandwich on whole wheat bread for lunch. Now I have brown rice instead of white with dinner and a cup of popcorn at snack time. I'm working on rejecting processed fare that is high in fat or sweeteners in favor of unprocessed, fiber-rich whole grains and produce; these foods, besides meeting our nutritional needs, seem to send a stronger signal to the brain that we've eaten enough.

We now have supermarkets full of low-fat yogurt, whole-grain bagels, and precut vegetables, so following a healthy diet can be as simple as steering your grocery cart down one or two aisles and skipping the rest.

Today, I will only worry about today. I will eat foods that are healthy for me. That's what I'll do today. If I eat something that doesn't feel good in my body, I'll put that on the list of items I won't be eating again soon.

What changes can you make in your diet that will help you feel healthy and maintain a healthy weight?

THE LONGEVITY TEST

Life is like a great jazz riff. You sense the end the very moment you were wanting it to go on forever.

—SHEILA BALLANTYNE

I took the longevity test in *Living to 100* by Thomas T. Perls and Margery Hutter Silver. My calculations tell me I could live to be ninety-five in fairly good health. Some of the factors that will help me do this are yes answers to: Do you drink a glass of red wine daily (+2)? Do you avoid the sun and use sunblock (+3)? Can you shed stress (+7)? It sounds like sitting peacefully in the shade with a glass of red wine is the way to go!

Now I'm thinking about what it means to live until I'm ninety-five. At this writing, I'm sixty-five, and according to the test, I've got approximately thirty more years as a resident of this planet. Decisions must be made, and I'm full of disturbing questions.

Do I get the chance to retire with my husband? Will we instead suffer the loss or illness of one of us, which would change the entire picture? Am I doing all I can do to stay healthy? Am I making the right decisions about health care? I say, do all you can to live a healthy life. Guarantees are not what life is about.

Today, I took the longevity test, and it appears I'm pretty healthy. I know I'm not 100 percent assured of living all the way to ninety-five, but I'll continue to make healthy lifestyle choices and enjoy the ride wherever it takes me.

What healthy decisions can you make starting today?

WHY SHOULD I EXERCISE?

My grandmother started walking five miles a day when she was sixty. She's ninety-seven now, and we don't know where the heck she is.

—Ellen DeGeneres

Let me assure you, I'm not an exercise guru or gym queen. I eat well and take daily vitamin supplements. I drag myself to the gym for aqua-size classes with consistent irregularity. I'm not trying to measure up to the media standards of the sleek, sweaty, rippling woman pumping away on the step machine. After birthing three children, I don't have any fantasies of having a washboard stomach. Basic maintenance and slowing the inevitable decline are my goals.

A well-developed exercise program not only reshapes and trims your body, but it also decreases your chances of heart attacks, osteoporosis, certain types of arthritis, and other conditions that creep up on us in our later years. For me, one of exercise's most valuable outcomes is the increase in endorphins—those valuable chemicals that produce an emotional high. Creating a steady supply of endorphins through regular exercise can do more for our bodies and our mental health during menopause and beyond than all the cosmetics and plastic surgery in the world.

Exercise can prolong your life regardless of heredity. Studies show that people who walked briskly, jogged, or did an equivalent exercise for thirty minutes at least six times a month had more than a 40 percent lower death rate than those who were sedentary. Another study of sedentary seniors ages sixty to sixty-five found that those who walked briskly for fifteen to forty-five minutes three times a week improved their performance on computer-related tasks compared with those who did one hour of just stretching and toning three times weekly. The extra flow of oxygen to the brain promoted by walking slows age-related decline in mental functioning. While social and intellectual activities can be beneficial in preventing Alzheimer's, physical exercise and strength training have been found to be even more beneficial.

After checking with your doctor, pick one or two exercises you like. The best exercise is the one you will continue to do regularly because it feels good. To stay motivated, we must each ask ourselves why we want to be fit. I exercise to maintain my muscular strength and balance so I won't become too dependent in my later years as well as to have the physical and mental energy to travel and to do things with my grandchildren.

What would motivate you to start an exercise program or to stay with the one you already have in place?

WHERE ARE MY GLASSES?

I am still surprised when I need my spectacles to read a menu or scan the telephone directory.

—MELODY BEATTIE

My glasses were never where I was when I needed them. Now, I have ten-dollar drugstore half-frame magnifying glasses placed all over my house. I love them so much that when one of the earpieces breaks off,

I don't throw them out. One pair with a broken arm hangs over the edge of the reading materials bin in the master bath. Another stands in the pencil cup in the kitchen for reading recipes, the ingredients list on the back of packaged foods, and the label on my vitamins. How come the take-as-directed information on the back of my age fifty-plus nutritional supplements is written in a typeface that only someone under thirty could read?

I'll never forget the time I was sitting across from one of my clients who had given me something to read. When I couldn't find my glasses, I got up and excused myself, saying I needed to go hunt for them. Before I could get out of my office my client rather shyly said, "Dr. Blair, you've got several pairs on you already." I had one pair tucked in the V neck of my sweater, and two pairs—one behind the other—perched on my head!

If you keep losing your glasses like I do, try attaching a strip of Velcro to your glasses case and the corresponding strip to your reading chair or nightstand and stick them on. Wear your glasses attached to a chain or cord hung around your neck. When you take them off, hang them on a hook you've installed near your desk or reading chair.

Keeping our eyes healthy is incredibly important. Get your eyes checked regularly for the following, even if you don't notice any problems:

- Presbyopia—changes in reading-distance vision

- Macular degeneration—deterioration of central vision

- Glaucoma—blurring of peripheral vision

- Cataract—cloudy eye lens and blurred or dim vision

There are benefits to not seeing as well as I did in my younger years, though. My house always looks dust free, and my wrinkles are harder to see. If you really don't want to worry about your aging face, just don't put your glasses on when you look in the mirror!

When was the last time you had your eyes checked? Do you need a new pair of glasses? A new prescription?

WHAT YOU DON'T "NO" CAN HURT YOU

More and more, I am claiming the fullness of my right to choose;
I am celebrating my freedom to be a woman saying NO!

—JANET QUINN

As young girls, we're conditioned to please others, and it doesn't take a little girl very long to realize that people-pleasing and self-sacrifice are a way to gain self-worth. As a result, we may often feel guilty when we get up the courage to say no to those who request our time and attention.

Saying no to the things that sap your energy will leave you time for the things that bring you fulfillment and happiness. Learn to say no without guilt. If you don't, you end up doing things you don't want to or shouldn't be doing—all the while acting, on the surface, as if everything is just fine.

Is someone in your life asking you to do something that compromises your self-respect or integrity or just doesn't feel right? Would fulfilling the other person's need take away from your sense of well-being? Does that person's request come at a bad time so that it detracts from your health and happiness? Are you in a pattern in which you are doing favors for, or giving to, others but getting very little in return?

As older, wiser women, we need to say a clear and definite yes to some uses of our time and a resounding no to others—our health depends on it! We need time that we regularly set aside without apology or explanation—time not easily given over to compromise.

Don't say yes right away to every request. It's okay to say that you need a few minutes, hours, or days to think about it. But remember that you're not making the other person wrong for asking; you are simply clear about your own needs.

Can you think of someone or something you need to start saying no to?

WHAT DID YOU SAY?

Maybe the reason our hearing diminishes after age fifty is because there are just some things we don't want to hear anymore. Like you're too old to roller skate!

—ALISON, AGE 59

About half of women over sixty-five have some degree of hearing loss but most don't know it. In fact, hearing loss ranks with heart disease as one of the most common physical problems in this age group. The loss occurs gradually, and in many cases, it goes unnoticed for years.

Warning signs include: voices get lost in background noise, you favor one ear, you get ringing or buzzing in the ears, you wonder why everyone is mumbling, you turn up the TV or radio volume until others complain, you need to look at people to understand what they're saying, and you may become socially withdrawn and avoid initiating conversations.

Can't hear but don't want a clunky hearing aid? Options now include in-the-ear-and-canal (less conspicuous than previous models), and completely in-the-canal (unnoticeable) models, in addition to behind-the-ear devices. An audiologist can help you find the right fit for your ear, your particular kind of hearing loss, and your budget. New hearing aids are now digital instead of analog; the result is better amplification of incoming sounds and an improved ability to handle background noise. Some even use an artificial intelligence system to distinguish speech from noise, and microchips so small they fit in the eye of a needle.

In talking about her loss of hearing in old age, actress Helen Hayes said, "Fighting as hard as we can against a disability is essential; we don't want to give in and give up. But denying it, for reasons of pride or prejudice, is a whole other matter."

Be aware of any hearing loss, and mention this to your doctor.

UTERUSES AND VAGINAS

I can't stand how grim everyone is about aging—osteoporosis, liver spots, vaginal dryness—oh, please!

—Valerie Harper

If you're an older woman, you have at least a vagina and maybe a uterus. These precious body parts deserve our attention just like any other body part. I'll start this discussion with our friend the vagina (Mom used to refer to it as *down there*).

When women enter menopause, one of the most common complaints is vaginal dryness during sex, which can make intercourse feel scratchy or painful. Medical science has come to the rescue. Talk to your gynecologist regarding prescriptions, lubricants, or hormone creams that can thicken and nourish the vaginal tissues.

Regular toning of your vaginal muscles increases circulation to this area of your body and helps keep vaginal tissues moist and healthy. Exercise your vaginal muscles by doing Kegel exercises. Squeeze your vaginal muscles (these are the same ones you use to stop the flow of urine), hold them for ten seconds, and relax. Repeat several times per day. You can do them while you're stopped at a traffic light or in line at the supermarket. Try not to contract your thighs, buttocks, or abdominals at the same time, and visualize *down there* as healthy, pink, moist, and resilient.

If you still have a uterus, you may be one of the 40 percent of US women who have uterine fibroids. These are tumors, usually noncancerous, that grow in the wall of the uterus. Some fibroids go away of their own accord, while others stay and cause problems. Although there are dietary and hormonal reasons behind why so many women have these growths, according to Dr. Christiane Northrup, the baseline energetic causes of fibroids may have to do with blockage and stagnation of the energy of the pelvis. She suggests, "The illnesses that originate in this area of the body are activated by prolonged stress from fear of losing control over our physical environments. . . . Fibroids represent creative energy that hasn't been birthed."

If you've had a hysterectomy or are anticipating one, remember that a hysterectomy doesn't necessarily diminish your sexuality. Most women report more sexual activity and greater pleasure after the operation than before it. The probable reason: the symptoms that usually lead to hysterectomy, including pain and heavy bleeding, keep women from fully enjoying sex before the operation.

So pay attention to those parts down there, and get on with living.

Is there anything you need to discuss with your gynecologist?

SLEEPING

Life is something that happens when you can't get to sleep.

—Fran Lebowitz

Some researchers say that lack of sleep may make you age faster. The lack seems to affect carbohydrate metabolism and endocrine function, which are effects that normally occur with aging. Just like air, food, and water, sleep is a basic necessity. But night sweats and arthritis pain might interrupt our sleep patterns. Sleep deprivation may increase the severity of other disorders as well.

On the other hand, don't worry if you don't get exactly eight hours of sleep a night, but see the doctor if you're regularly sleeping more than nine hours or less than six. The unbroken, sound sleep of youth is a thing of the past for most older women. Doctors say this is a normal change with age. It's neither good nor bad, but this change worries many women when it shouldn't.

Sometimes other factors keep us from sleeping well. Nothing seems to affect an otherwise happy relationship like the rumble of a freight train coming from the pillow next to you. If snoring is keeping you awake, I think sleeping in separate beds can help the relationship. Chronic lack of sleep can make us irritable, affect concentration and judgment, and even harm a marriage. The objective is to have as healthy a relationship as possible when awake. If sleeping separately improves the daytime relationship, then do it.

We may become angry at our partners, but snorers have no control over their noisemaking, and it may be a sign of obstructive sleep apnea, a serious threat to health. Instead of getting angry, encourage them to seek medical help.

Snoring aside, here are some helpful tips for getting a good night's sleep:

- Establish a regular bedtime schedule.

- Create a comfortable bed. Buy a good mattress and comfy sheets.

- Exercise regularly, but not within two or three hours of bedtime.

- Make your bedroom conducive to sleep.

- Keep your bedroom at an optimal temperature and noise level.

- Take a warm bath.

- Do yoga, listen to peaceful music, or meditate.

- Do some light reading.

- Turn off the TV.

- Write your worries in a journal and close it.

- Set regular times for sleeping and waking, and try not to vary from the schedule.

- Avoid caffeine, alcohol, and tobacco products before bedtime.

- Don't eat a lot, but have a light snack so hunger doesn't keep you up.

What can you do to create a better night's sleep?

PHYSICAL DISABILITY

Healing always happens when I choose to remember to be a woman being gentle with myself.

—Janet F. Quinn

A few years ago, I opted to have my painful bunions corrected. (*Bunion* sounds like a funny vegetable, a cross between an onion and a bump.) Bunions are the result of a serious foot deformity, a misalignment of bones. In my case, the surgeon made a seven-inch incision, sliced open the bumpy onion, took out a hunk of bone, inserted some screws and wires to keep the newly formed foot in place, sewed me up, and sent me off in a clunky, splinted boot cast with Velcro closings. He told me not to put any weight on my toes, to walk on my heel, to keep the foot elevated, and to take the painkillers when I needed them. His last words were "see you in a week; the hard cast stays on for a month."

My first shower after the surgery was a humbling experience. My husband assisted me by wrapping the cast in garbage bags. He got a good look at my cellulite legs and blubbery bottom as he positioned me in the shower, standing by in case I slipped and fell. I felt like a child again—or an old, old lady dependent on a home health-care aide for necessary body care and maintenance.

I was grateful to have a husband to care for me. I imagine what it would be like without one—alone and needing paid strangers to come into my home, viewing my cellulite. I imagine what it would be like to live in a country without doctors who do this kind of surgery. I imagine what it would be like not to have the option to correct my foot because I lacked insurance or resources.

I tried not to be distracted by the throbbing pain, stinging incision, and swelling going on underneath the bandages. I tried not to be a whiny baby or a spoiled brat, and I counted my blessings.

Take a moment of gratitude for the health you do have.

HEART HEALTH

You have double the risk of having a heart attack for two hours after getting angry!

—Mary Ann Mayo

Women are twice as likely as men to die after one heart attack, and those who survive are more likely to have a second heart attack within four years. Have I scared you enough?

I bet you didn't know that marital difficulties can increase a woman's risk of heart attack. A woman who has had a heart attack or other acute cardiac episode, and whose marital difficulties include substance abuse, infidelity, economic difficulties, or a partner's illness, is more likely to suffer another episode.

Here are some other interesting heart facts that I've collected from a wide variety of reliable sources such as the *Harvard Heart Letter*:

- According to nutritionists, chocolate is good for your heart. One ounce of dark chocolate contains ten times more antioxidants than one ounce of strawberries. Even better, a diet that includes one ounce of chocolate per day seems to increase HDL (that's the good cholesterol) and to prevent LDL (bad cholesterol) from oxidizing—one of the possible contributing factors for heart disease.

- One study showed that a cup of black tea a day was enough to lower heart attack risk by 44 percent, and another study said six cups of tea every day could reduce stroke risk by 42 percent.

- Heart attacks are seasonal. They peak during December and January, when there are 33 percent more deaths from heart attacks than in summer and early fall. The reasons could be increased food, alcohol, and salt consumption; additional stress; respiratory infections; and reduced hours of daylight.

- Women who eat nutritious meals, exercise daily, and don't smoke have reduced their risk of heart disease by as much as 82 percent.

- Optimistic people who have had heart attacks are less likely to suffer subsequent heart problems, and their recovery is almost three times faster.

The *Journal of the American Heart Association* says always call 911 if you feel you are having a heart attack. The faster you get to the hospital, the better your chances are for successful treatment.

A woman's symptoms of heart attack are not the same as those for men. Women may experience chest, stomach, or abdominal pain that does not necessarily feel acute or crushing, nausea or dizziness, shortness of breath, heart palpitations, fatigue, or a general feeling of weakness. Doctors recommend that if you are having symptoms of heart attack, you should chew a full-strength aspirin and get to the hospital as soon as possible.

These days, having heart disease is not an automatic death sentence—it's a call to action. A time to make changes. A time to get off the couch, get moving, and discover the joy of living.

What steps can you take starting today to protect your heart?

HEALING PETS

Animals are our spiritual companions, living proof of a simply abundant source of love.

—Sarah Ban Breathnach

The bond we form with pets can make an enormous difference to our health—sometimes the difference between life and death. Research reveals that pet owners are less likely than people without pets to develop heart disease and that pet owners who have heart attacks live longer than coronary attack victims without pets. Pet owners of all ages go to their doctors less often, have more fun, and feel more secure than those who have no pets. Pets like dogs and cats can help control blood pressure, and some studies show that a pet's calming influence is better at controlling high blood pressure than antihypertension drugs.

Nursing homes report that when they bring animals into their environments, patient death rates drop by an amazing 40 percent and the need for medication decreases, too.

If you don't want the long-term commitment of a pet or can't afford to own one, you can take advantage of a wonderful volunteer opportunity through your local animal shelter or humane society. If you are willing to commit to a two- to six-week situation, you can be a foster parent for lost or rescued pets needing a place to stay while they recover from minor illness or because they are too young yet for adoption. If you have allergies, look for a dog like a labradoodle that doesn't cause them.

Author Carolyn G. Heilbrun wrote, "No one who has not, upon returning from any absence, long or short, been greeted by a loving dog can understand what devotion is." Whether from the need for affection, company, or health, consider bringing a pet into your life.

If you don't already have a pet, what kind of pet do you see yourself with in the future (if any)?

DON'T FALL DOWN!

Our greatest glory is not in never falling, but in rising every time we fall.

—CONFUCIUS

According to Margaret Gottschalk, a research physical therapist, most falls are not random or an inevitable part of aging. Older adults who are physically inactive lose muscle mass and strength more quickly than active individuals who participate in strength training. Sixty-year-olds who maintain sedentary lifestyles will, at the age of seventy, be up to 50 percent weaker than they were at the age of sixty.

I live in a house that was built in 1928. As opposed to modern houses where the washer and dryer are more conveniently located, my machines are down a flight of steep wooden stairs ending in a poured-concrete basement floor. I've been thinking more and more about how it would feel to fall down those stairs (or up them) with no one around to see or hear me tumble. With this in mind, I have vowed to keep up my strength and balance exercises.

Most falls by seniors at home are not caused by household hazards but by weak muscles, in addition to bad eyesight (I avoid walking in my bifocals) and poorly constructed shoes. Very few falls are associated with commonly recognized potential hazards, such as loose rugs and slippery bathtubs. But just in case, put nonskid tape on the edges of steps and nonskid mats on hard floors and in tubs and showers.

The best way for us to avoid falls is to strengthen muscles, improve balance, preserve vision, wear appropriate footwear, monitor the effects of medication, and remove potential hazards.

Health and age-related changes that contribute to falls include arthritis and decreased sensation in the feet, known as peripheral neuropathy. The other major cause of falls is hazardous conditions in the home environment. Fortunately, there are numerous ways to reduce these hazards for yourself or a loved one. Many of them involve little or no cost.

Keep floors clear of small objects and loose wires. Scatter rugs are dangerous, stairways should be well lit, and night-lights are a must in the bathroom. Wear shoes that provide solid support. Keep stairs free of clutter. As you walk down stairs, go slowly and keep at least one hand free to hold the railing, or install a second handrail and use both hands. Take off your reading glasses when walking around, and always keep your regular glasses clean. Eliminate throw rugs.

In the kitchen, keep the pots, dishes, and staple foods you use regularly within easy reach. Store the heaviest items in the lower cupboards. If you must reach high places, get a step stool that has a high handrail and rubber tips. Never use a chair. In the bedroom keep a lamp within easy reach of your bed and a flashlight on hand in case there's a power failure. Keep a phone at your bedside. If balance becomes an ongoing problem, consider a cane or walker.

Have someone install grab bars by the toilet and in the bathtub or shower area if you need them. Use a rubber mat with suction cups in the tub or shower, and a nonskid bath mat on the floor. Consider a bathtub seat or shower chair and a handheld showerhead so you can shower sitting down. Buy a raised toilet seat if you have trouble getting on and off the toilet.

You may want to sign on with a personal emergency response service, whereby you wear a small, lightweight, waterproof pendant or bracelet that has a button to press to alert medical professionals if you run into trouble or fall.

Above all, the most important action to take to prevent falling is regular exercise. Older women participating in regular exercise have fewer injuries from falls, as weight training increases bone density and reaction time.

What are you willing to do to prevent falls in your home?

COFFEE AND THE PEE-PEE DANCE

The Cycle of Life: At age 4 success is not peeing your pants. . . . At age 80 success is . . . not peeing your pants.

—Unknown

Lifetime coffee lovers should rejoice. Two to three cups daily may boost your life span, as the antioxidant compounds in coffee curb the inflammation that may lead to cardiovascular disease and caffeine may offset some types of age-related mental decline.

Well, it's nice that someone discovered that we can increase our mental abilities by drinking coffee. But does that increased mental ability assist you in making all those trips to the bathroom? And what about the trips to the bathroom that you don't quite make? Have you ever done the pee-pee dance or the cross-legged bunny hop on your way to relieve yourself?

If you're a coffee lover, you probably enjoy stopping for a nice hot cup at a diner while you're on an extended car trip, only to regret it thirty minutes later. Have you ever sped into a gas station, left the car running, jumped out, and dashed to the ladies' room only to find the door locked? I have. I nearly knocked someone over in the station's food mart while grabbing for the key suspended by a wood block at the cash register.

Bladder control problems are neither an inevitable part of aging nor a disease but rather a problem that can be managed. Ask your doctor or gynecologist about medication to help you with this issue. Visit the bathroom on a regular basis. Cut down on your caffeine consumption. My morning coffee is now a half-and-half mix of caffeinated and decaffeinated coffees. And when I'm on the road, I avoid coffee and sodas with caffeine altogether.

Make some small changes, and you can still enjoy your occasional cup of coffee without having to do the pee-pee dance or mop the floor on the way to the bathroom.

If you've got this issue, what small changes can you make?

CHEW ON THIS

Life is short. Smile while you still have teeth.

—Mallory Hopkins

Boy, was I surprised to find out that I needed periodontal work. I needed to have oral surgery—cut and sew my gums. Yikes! Thank God for laughing gas. Have I scared you enough? Sorry. But this is important, and I have to get your attention. The good news is, flossing and regular deep cleaning in the dentist's chair can help prevent it. However, some of us (like me) have simply inherited weak gums.

One positive trend among the aging population is the increasing attention to dental and oral health, and seniors are making more regular visits to the dentist. Despite the improvements, problems remain. A report from the Department of Health and Human Services found that one-third of seniors with natural teeth have untreated dental cavities in their crowns or roots. Bummer!

As you age, your mouth will get drier or medications may cause your mouth to dry out. The less saliva you have, the more quickly bacteria can build up, and you become more prone to gum issues and bad breath.

Let me say it again—floss. See your dentist regularly. He or she can also check for oral cancer. Have your teeth deep cleaned at least once a year. You'll improve the odds of keeping your own teeth into very old age, and wouldn't that be nice? Keeping your gums healthy could even prevent a heart attack because periodontal disease is a risk factor for cardiovascular problems.

I'm sorry I scared you a bit, but if you want to eat more than applesauce and oatmeal in your later years, take good care of your teeth and gums.

What steps can you take to improve your oral health?

BREASTS

This last and significant passage of my life, my aging, deserves my full attention and devotion.

—Ruth Raymond Thone

Breast cancer is a big fear in older women, and although 90 percent of us will never develop it, there is still every reason in the world to protect yourself as best you can. Maybe you go for your mammogram according to the recommended schedule. But maybe you don't. Or if you do, you dread it. Maybe you resist going because it feels like having your breasts pressed between two large encyclopedias.

I recently found out about something called a comfort pad. This thin foam rubber pad attaches to the metal squeeze plates and comes in various sizes to accommodate most women. The result is a much more tolerable exam. Not every mammogram facility offers these wonderful pads, but do take the time to ask if they have them available.

If they find something, consider what Dr. Oz says: "If you're weighing a lumpectomy versus a mastectomy, you need to step into the doctor's office prepared for a conversation about the risks of operating again after a lumpectomy." He says a second surgery is emotionally, financially, and physically stressful, and reoperation may delay important drug or radiation treatments.

If you've experienced a suspicious lump or been treated for breast cancer, please nag the rest of us to take our breast health seriously. You've been there. We'll listen to you. Tell your story to every woman who will listen. Offer to go to a screening with someone who is fearful. You may help save a life.

What are you willing to do to promote your breast health or that of someone else?

MEDICAL DIRECTIVES

It's a comfort knowing someone I've chosen would speak for me when I can't speak for myself.

—JOAN, AGE 71

The AARP suggests we have a medical directive in place just in case. Considering and implementing what they suggest may bring up denial and avoidance. It did for me. Who wants to think about and plan ahead for the worst? Then again, I imagine myself in a coma trying to kick myself because I hadn't done anything to put important medical directives in place.

So here's what I did. I did one of the things on the list of suggestions below every month or so. It took me about a year to put it all together because it was an emotional overload—denial and avoidance. Now I'm glad I got it done.

- Discuss your wishes with family members, doctors, and caregivers.

- Consult an attorney about a living will.

- Avoid generic advance directive forms; compile and update documents with your doctor's input.

- Sign each directive, date it, and have it witnessed according to the laws in your state.

- Pick a health care agent or proxy who will act aggressively on your behalf; the person closest to you may not always be the best.

- Put copies of your advance directives in your medical records, and make them widely available to family and care providers.

- Put a plan in place and get on with the joy of living.

What steps are you willing to take to make sure your medical directives are honored when the time comes?

part III

10
our living spaces

These next years are going to be about creating a life, and a living space that serves me and reflects my true nature.

—JOYCE, AGE 63

The creation of an authentic living space is a process of self-discovery and one that deepens over time. Many of us spent years investing in and making a home for our families—living room furniture coated in Teflon; indestructible, dirt-resistant Berber carpets; bedroom dressers from garage sales; and playrooms decorated in pink Barbie furniture. Family or not, we may have spent half our lives in surroundings that didn't quite reflect our true nature.

As we age, some changes are inevitable in the environment in which we live. The homes that served us well may now be too expensive, too large, and too difficult to keep up. We crave a simpler, safer, and more beautiful life now.

Some of us will resist leaving our homes and communities and choose to age in place. Aging in place will make sense to some of us, especially if we can learn how to accept support from friends and neighbors.

I talked with quite a few older women before I wrote this section. Aging in their own home was a goal for a number of the independent type. Others told me they couldn't wait to get out from under the responsibility of a house that was too big or away from a deteriorating community. Some women told me they were ready to move and their husbands weren't; others had no vision of when or where they would go.

Some days, aging in place resonates with me—then winter comes, and my sidewalks and stairs become ski slopes, and the ice builds up on my driveway and in my gutters and in my bones, and the dreary, sunless days grab at my throat. Like many older people who are leaving a home where they raised their children, tended the garden, repaired the screens, and redecorated the bathroom, I will leave with a heavy heart. I think positive thoughts like how liberating it will be to clean out and throw out the accumulation of stuff in my basement and attic. I fantasize about connecting with other like-minded folks and building new friendships, living new adventures in new places.

Hopefully, this section will assist you in exploring your feelings and acquiring knowledge that will enable you to make the choices you will need to make.

THOUGHTS ON AUNT GRACE

You may be wondering what Buddhism has to do with growing older, but if you can accept that "non-attachment" is helpful, you will discover that possessions aren't as important as they were.

—REBECCA LATIMER

My husband's Aunt Grace was someone I admired for who she was and how she lived her life. She was widowed for some time and living alone at ninety, and we often visited her in her small, tastefully appointed one-bedroom apartment in the upscale neighborhood of Central Park West in Manhattan. On one of our visits, I noticed something inspirational about her lifestyle. She had enough money to buy out Saks Fifth Avenue, yet when she opened her front hall closet door to retrieve her coat for a walk with us to the grocery store, I noticed only these few items:

Getting Older Better

- An umbrella

- A raincoat

- A lightweight coat for spring

- A heavy woolen coat for winter

- One pair of sturdy, fashionable overshoes

- One silk scarf and one woolen scarf

- One pair of well-made leather gloves

This was a woman who could afford to fill her closets three times over! I never asked her why she didn't have an accumulation of things, but if I had, I'm sure she would have responded that living in a simple, uncluttered apartment made life much easier and more manageable.

Aunt Grace had a small, simple kitchen with no fancy appliances— just the basics. She and several of her older neighbors checked in on each other daily. Grace loved being around people, culture, and the arts, so Manhattan suited her. No retirement home for her! In fact, she lived happily on her own in her apartment until she died in her mid-nineties.

In your journal, write about an older woman whose lifestyle you admire.

STAYING IN YOUR HOME

The people who are flourishing today are people who are planning for 40 or 50 more years of life after they hit midlife.

—GAIL SHEEHY

Despite our hopes of staying in our homes forever, many of us are without the necessary amenities to do so. We tend to focus on our needs for the next five years or so but neglect what we'll need later in life. We have to be realistic. You will need to consider what architectural features will make your house elder friendly as well as those community characteristics and services that will help you continue to live in your home.

Some of the changes and modifications you will need to consider include installing grab bars in bathrooms, levers (instead of doorknobs), nonslip flooring, an emergency alert system, wide doorways, and entrances without steps. A bedroom and full bath on the main level make it easier for you to live on one floor. A safe neighborhood is important and so is living near a hospital or other health care facility with a grocery or drugstore nearby.

When the time comes, the community should offer transportation—preferably door-to-door—home-delivered meals, and services that offer to do errands and chores.

Another way to stay in your house is multigenerational living. There are younger women who need housing who would gratefully live alongside you in your own home. Some may provide you with cleaning help, companionship, and transportation in exchange for a place to live.

Take care of identifying and installing some of what you need now to stay in your home in the future. Then sit back, relax, and enjoy your life.

If you want to stay in your home for the rest of your life, what steps can you take now to make that a reality?

GARDENING AND GROWING

The garden is growth and change and that means loss as well as constant new treasures to make up for a few disasters.

—MAY SARTON

I am, I imagine, a farmer at heart. At the very least, I am a gardener. Today, after weeding the garden and picking tomatoes, I washed the earthworm-scented soil from my hands and reverently placed the ripened tomatoes, oversized zucchini, and herbs in the sink to be washed.

I love the smell of fresh herbs and vegetables simmering in olive oil and garlic on a fall evening. This is the reward for hard work and a tortured back.

Just when I thought there would inevitably come a time when I'd have to limit my farming activities, I found three articles that inspired me to keep on digging. One of them described an eighty-one-year-old woman who had been gardening for sixty years and kept in shape by exercising five times a week so she could keep up with her garden. She had a healthy attitude and believed that you can't expect to keep everything perfect. She suggested that you let some wildflowers grow, relax, and enjoy the weeds. I read a newspaper article about Fran Dalton, age seventy-one, who grows giant pumpkins (eight hundred–plus pounds) in her secret hideaway garden plot in Newburyport, Massachusetts. She uses a special compost mixture, which she hauls to her plot and tills by hand.

Gardening can help women fifty and over build stronger bones, to the point that working in the garden for one hour a week is almost as effective for building bone strength as weight lifting. Of course, you should begin gradually and get a bone density test to see how much you can do without risking injury. If your doctor advises against doing strenuous gardening, consider growing and nurturing houseplants as an alternative.

If you don't have space for an outdoor garden (or don't want one) here are a few suggestions:

- Inside your house or apartment, create mini-gardens with plants, water, and rocks.

- By a window, place a bowl of water or a small fountain, and surround it with houseplants.

- If space is limited, induce the bulbs of paper-whites, tulips, daffodils, hyacinths, or crocuses in bowls filled with gravel or small stones.

- Place a bird feeder outside your window.

- Become a member of a community garden, or volunteer to help a friend with hers.

As you plant and nurture a garden, you nurture your mind, body, and spirit as well. Gardening can also reduce stress and help control anxiety. It frees the mind and connects you with spirit.

What can you do to connect with the earth and with growing things?

COLOR YOUR WORLD (FENG SHUI)

No matter our decorating style—realized or aspired to—the essential spiritual grace our homes should possess is the solace of comfort.

—SARAH BAN BREATHNACH

When you move to a smaller place or a retirement community, this is the perfect opportunity to consider how the placement of furniture and the colors in your environment play a part in your life energy. The chaotic environmental energies we were able to deal with when we were younger may not be suited to us now. Conscious awareness regarding our personal space is extremely important, especially as we age. We need all the positive energy we can muster.

Consider the principles of *feng shui,* Chinese for "geomancy"—the art of placement. It's a three-thousand-year-old system that analyzes and corrects the flow of energy, the life force—or chi—within a home or office. Harmonizing a home according to feng shui principles makes us feel welcome when we come home, where we remember who we are.

According to these principles, the energy blockages in our spaces affect our lives, our futures, and our health. Obstacles in our pathway affect our comings and goings in life. If a door doesn't open fully, feng shui says we're not opening to the fullness of the room. Dripping faucets leak out energy, affecting our finances because water represents wealth. Windows are the eyes of the home, so not seeing out is an obstacle to energy flow because we are unable to see the world. Healthy plants can help raise the life force within the home.

Color reflects emotional energy and can help us get what we want from our surroundings. It can mirror feelings or free them. For example, pink in the bedroom is for nurturing, with a touch of red somewhere to bring out your warmth and put some passion into your life. Green is the color of strength and new growth.

You can improve the quality of your life by becoming aware of the subtle influences in your environment. The environment becomes a metaphor for the circumstances of our lives. If our house is a mess, so might be the quality of our thinking, or the condition of our relationships. Your home, big or small, can be decorated with beautiful, well-chosen pictures and lush plants, all expressing a clean, uncluttered simplicity.

Look around your home. Can you use some of the principles of feng shui in your current environment?

SOULFUL LIVING SPACE

Whenever we're inordinately dismal or fearful about aging, it means we've neglected life's spiritual dimension.

—MARSHA SINETAR

What feeling would you like in your house or apartment? Architects and builders may ask about your requirements for kitchen appliances, closet space, and other physical necessities, but they seldom inquire about the qualities of soul you would like expressed in the design. These next years are meant to be soul-filled years, and it's difficult to feel connected to your soul in an environment that doesn't support you in that growth.

Surrounded by technological comforts, many women long for a way of life that encourages enrichment and meaning. At this time in particular, you may be searching for inspiration and a sense of sacredness that is natural, practical, personal, and immediate. Something as simple as the sound of water gurgling in the bathtub, sunlight spilling on the windowsill, flowers scenting the air, and numerous other experiences invite soul to enter the rooms of our homes.

Soulful living is tied to life's particular moments, such as savoring good food, engaging in meaningful conversation, spending time with genuine friends, and having experiences that touch the heart. Our homes provide the setting for those moments that warm a deep place in us. A home for the soul is not the result of a particular style or design—the primary ingredient in creating a home for the soul is our conscious attention.

Creating space that supports our need to be in soul-filled solitude is also important. If possible, create a space for meditation, prayer, study, writing, drawing, and playing music—a place where the mind and body can settle into the luminous silence of our true nature. Creating a setting in order to let go of demands and obligations gives us space to regain our center and be replenished by our inner resources.

Can you make your home into a more soulful living space?

SIMPLIFYING

Anything that doesn't qualify as either pleasurable or useful doesn't deserve house room.

—JOAN CLEVELAND

How many times have you been seduced into buying one more appliance to supposedly make your life easier, one more gadget that promises to save time, one more trinket to adorn your wrist or fingers, one more garage sale item to clutter your coffee table? As you get older, you may not have the physical and emotional stamina to keep it all in order.

At sixty-five, it feels like I've finally gotten life down to its essence. The superfluous has been stripped away, and it's a relief to see it go. It takes work to simplify, and once it's done, it feels wonderful.

The biggest step you can take in simplifying your life is to own fewer objects. There's a natural tendency to believe that possessing more things will make us happy. But the things we own also take energy and resources—in a sense, they own us. They require us to spend money to buy and maintain them; we must expend effort to tend them.

Take an inventory of all your possessions. Identify those that add value to your life and give you pleasure and those that don't. Consider getting rid of those items that cost more in time, trouble, dusting, or money to maintain than they are worth. Throwing them in the trash is an option, but I prefer recycling them: sell them in a yard sale, auction them on the Internet, give them to family and friends, or donate them to charity. Ah, freedom!

In terms of stuff, how can you simplify your life?

PAINT AND WALLPAPER

Several years ago . . . I announced that I was too old ever to hang wallpaper again, and if things got too shabby we'd have to bring in a professional.

—MADELEINE L'ENGLE

When I was in my energetic early thirties, I did much of the work on my then well-worn 1928 home by myself. Climbing up and down ladders, I painted inside and out, hung wallpaper (badly), laid flooring, and refinished and assembled furniture. Now just looking at the ladder and work gloves in the basement makes me want to take a nap.

I'm still living in that dear old house, and some of the work I did twenty years ago now needs to be done again. Refinished wooden floors lose their shine; bathroom tiles turn dull; and greenish, dated wallpaper saddens a room. These things get me down and steal my energy if I let them go too long.

Like me, you may not have the strength or balance to climb a ladder or paint a room, but how much energy does it take to pick up the phone and ask someone to paint a room for you? If you've always maintained and nurtured your home in the past as I have, it may be hard to let go and let someone else help with the necessary upkeep.

You don't have to do it all yourself. I find it a lot safer and a great deal more entertaining to sit and watch others do it for me or to leave the house and come back to find it done!

Make a list of friends, family, or professionals you can trust to help make your environment clean, safe, and attractive.

SELLING YOUR HOME

If we are still trying to figure out how to care for our too large house and garden, and what to do with all our goods and chattels, we can't let go into a new life.

—Marion Woodman

Sometime in the future, you may have to move to a place where there aren't as many steps or rooms to keep up, or where there are facilities or relatives nearby in case you need them—where the cost of living is easier on your budget, where you can walk to the supermarket, where there are people your own age.

In preparation for a future time, I am cleaning, sorting, and throwing away things today. As my husband and I age, or I am widowed, someday the house I live in will need to be sold. Perhaps you're thinking about it, too. So I'm downsizing now—simplifying—while I still have the energy and a solid mind for organizing.

If it's time to sell your home, there are some simple things you can do to help sell it a bit faster:

- Out front: Look at your house from the street. If you need to, get someone to help you trim the hedges and bushes. Then add a coat of semigloss paint to the front door and buy a brand-new doormat. Polish the doorknob.

- Out back: Clean up the patio and deck. Repair or get rid of broken, discolored outdoor furniture.

- Foyer: Unclutter the entryway, and hang a mirror. Mirrors can help any room look more spacious. Consider putting a vase of fresh flowers on an entryway table to greet potential buyers.

- Dining room: Remove the leaves from your dining room table to make the room look bigger.

- Kitchen: Take down the refrigerator magnets and the grandkids' drawings from the refrigerator door, and put away the large countertop appliances.

Get rid of as much clutter as possible before putting your house on the market. An uncluttered house looks larger and more attractive to buyers.

What can you start doing now to make your home more desirable and easier to sell when the time comes?

RETIREMENT LIVING SPACES

We can't rely on others to plan our retirement, because each of us has our own unique realm where we want to be.

—MARION E. HAYNES

We all seek a level of comfort in our lives. We desire living where we want to live, doing things we enjoy doing, and experiencing something in the world that brings us a sense of satisfaction.

It may seem too soon to consider where to live in retirement, especially when you are strong and healthy, energetic, and living comfortably in a community where you have good support services, friends, and family. However, this is a very good time to investigate possible future living arrangements. You don't want to delay the search until you're sick, injured, or have lost a husband or partner who could have been helpful in the decision-making process. Take your time, and the search may even end up being enjoyable.

If you are like most women contemplating retirement and relocation, there are things to consider that might affect your quality of life, such as: where the children and grandchildren are living, housing costs, climate, economics, health care, personal safety, and access to recreational and cultural activities. You can do a lot of your search online. Here's a good resource: the Retirement Living Information Center (*www.retirementliving.com*) can help you choose from one of six types of facilities, and then you can search by city and state. You can get information about the nearest city, the weather there, maps, and other details.

I think it's a good idea to take a long, hard look into the future and not be caught off guard. Of course, life is unpredictable, but don't you want to be a participant in the process of life and have a say in where you spend your days?

Where do you see yourself living in retirement? Where would you feel most at home?

DOWNSIZING: PREPARING A MOVE TO A SMALLER, MORE MANAGEABLE HOME

I got rid of roomfuls of possessions and moved from a big house to a condominium . . . and I have felt much lighter of heart and mind since.

—ELAINE ST. JAMES

It may feel uncomfortable to think about, but as we age, creating a manageable living environment is a necessity. It may be time to consider moving to a smaller, more manageable home that better suits your needs. Maybe you've been banging around in a large, overwhelming, outdated place for too long and you're good and ready to make the change.

I find myself worrying from time to time about how I'll make the transition. Will I be able to create the kind of nurturing nest I know I'll require for my sunset years, a place that will support my body, mind, and spirit? Author Louise L. Hay wrote an affirmation we can all live by: "I provide myself a comfortable home, one that fills all my needs and is a pleasure to be in. I fill the rooms with the vibration of love so that all who enter, myself included, will feel the love and be nourished by it." I think that's where I'll start. When the time comes, I'll fill my new home with the vibration of love and let it happen from there.

I know there are lots of things that I will gladly let go of, the kind of material stuff that depletes my life force. Author Melody Beattie wrote, "Objects have energy, they have energy in them when we obtain them, and they have the energy and meaning we attribute to them. Choose carefully the possessions you want around you, for they tell a story all day long."

Make a conscious effort not to buy stuff you will later have to make space for in a smaller home, or stuff you will have to get rid of when the time comes. The act of letting go of the burden of caring for too many possessions will leave more room to fill your home with the vibration of love. Check out the National Association of Senior Move Managers at *www.nasmm.org.*

If you decide to move to a smaller, more manageable home someday, how would you like it to look and feel?

LIVING ALONE AND LIKING IT

When I am an old, old woman I may very well be
living all alone like many another before me.

—KATE BARNES

Thirty-six percent of women over age sixty-five live alone, and about 45 percent of the total population of older Americans are single. Chances are, you may find yourself living alone one day and wondering how to make the best of it.

Two of my favorite authors have positive thoughts on this topic. Frances Weaver says, "Living alone means I can eat all of the Pepperidge Farm cookies without feeling I must hide the empty sack." Carolyn. G. Heilbrun writes, "The solitude of old age is often pleasurable, offering, I sometimes think, a pleasure similar to those described by converts to a religion."

If you don't want to live alone, what alternatives do you have? What would it be like to live with your children, or to live in the company of other younger people? Intergenerational living has its drawbacks. Difficulties can arise from trying to combine what are essentially two different cultures. Members of the younger generation may move nonstop in all they do and find that you move too slowly. No matter how much you love and care for each other, your patience might get exhausted.

The old are younger in each other's presence. We need to be with others like us, others who understand our unreliable memories and our need for routine. Of course, it can be refreshing to visit with our younger family members, children, and friends. But isn't it a relief when they leave? Author Barbara Holland wrote, "No doubt about it, solitude is improved by being voluntary. . . . If you live with other people, their temporary absence can be refreshing."

My sister, Marilyn, who lived alone for many years, came up with some innovative advice for caring for yourself when you live alone:

- Have the newspaper delivered daily. The regularity of that event each morning can make you mindful of the things in life you can count on.

- Get an electric coffeepot with a timer. Set it the night before, and wake to the scent of coffee or tea as a welcoming way to start your day. You can do the same with a programmable bread maker.

- Plan in advance to have neighborhood youngsters shovel snow for you in the winter or weed for you in the summer. Make a snack for them during a break and have a chat.

- Install night-lights in every room of the house. Especially useful are the ones that come on automatically as the house dims.

- Buy yourself flowers—some beautiful bundles are affordably priced at the grocery store.

- Use aromatherapy to enhance your feelings of well-being and relaxation.

- Play beautiful music as you soak in a hot bathtub with bubbles up to your chin.

- Plug in a small TV in the kitchen. It's good company.

- Adopt a pet from the shelter—it will love you unconditionally.

- Buy a portable heat dish—an efficient space heater—to warm your damp or winter days, and take it from room to room with you.

- Skype, FaceTime, or email friends and family.

- Replace your old scratchy, polyester-blend sheets with soft cotton or flannel. Wash them and toss them in the dryer with a great-smelling fabric softener. Invest in a down comforter or feather bed so you feel like you're sleeping on a cloud in the arms of love.

- Invite a friend to your house for lunch or dinner at least once a week.

- When you're out in the world, smile a lot, and people will smile back at you.

Living alone is an opportunity to get to know yourself better, to get in touch with your inner resources. And living alone is a choice, not a sentence.

When (or if) you live alone, how would you like your life to be?

EMPTY NESTS WITH SILVER LININGS

I've reached the stage where I'm no longer able to call myself middle-aged because that's what my children are.

—Judith Viorst

The children are doing okay on their own, and the nest is empty. For some of you, the nest is empty because you were caregiving one or both of your parents who are no longer living with you. Or you are now living without your spouse.

This is an opportunity to create a space that is uniquely your own. One room to call your very own. One corner of the apartment reclaimed. One whole house to design any way you wish. Not only can you redesign your environment, but you can eat what and when you'd like, walk around naked after your shower, and surf the TV channels

Getting Older Better

whenever you're in the mood. You can fill your home with friends who like to drink martinis; you can play your music loud.

When (or if) the time comes that your nest is empty, what do you imagine doing in and with the newly acquired space?

CLUTTER: YOU CAN'T TAKE IT WITH YOU!

A regular, serious attack on mess and unnecessary clutter . . . makes you feel in control of all the parts of your life you care about.

—ALEXANDRA STODDARD

We spend the first half of our lives collecting and buying stuff and the second half of our lives trying to get rid of it all! Are you at risk for burial under an avalanche of stuff each time you open a closet door? Author Mary C. Morrison once remarked that although our houses may be empty of people, they are still full of an accumulation of things, and "our lives are encrusted with possessions and burdened with the work they entail."

I've been asking myself if I want my children to have to row through a sea of clutter when I'm gone. I imagine the burden it would create for them. "Who wants Mom's drawerful of candle stubs?" "Who wants Mom's vintage 1970s blouses?" (I've been hoping they would come back in style.) "Who wants Mom's stained linen napkins?" (I've been waiting until I had enough of them to put in a dark dye bath to hide the stains.) You may not have children, but consider the fact that your partner, other family members, or friends will eventually have to deal with your stuff.

My goal each day is to find one item to donate, throw out, or give away. It's amazing how many things I've been holding on to that are no longer of use. When we're ready to get real about our clutter, organizing gurus tell us that we should create three bags or boxes labeled *Garbage, Give Away,* and *Put Someplace Else* as well as a fourth that says

Undecidable. They suggest visiting your undecidable box after a few weeks and tossing or giving away anything you haven't retrieved in that time. My system is to keep a shopping bag behind my bedroom door, and the minute I have the thought, *Why am I holding on to this?,* into the donation bag it goes.

What can you do today to begin letting go and lightening up?

LEAVING HOME

At sixty-seven, I'm selfish enough to want my own way. I want to be with my own generation, people who understand the issues I live with. . . . So I live in a home with lots of people my age.

—"Bertha" age 67

It's a quiet Sunday afternoon. As I look out at the familiar views from each window of the house I've lived in for the past thirty years, I wonder how much I'll miss it when I need to move from here. Some days, I imagine I'll shoot a photograph out each of the windows and assemble the pictures into an album that I can take with me. I know that the next step in my evolution will need to be taken with courage.

Some of the older women I've met along the way were devastated when they had to leave their homes and go into an assisted living or long-term residential care facility. A series of upheavals had brought them to this part of the journey—their health was uncertain or they had lost their economic independence, and they usually had no options for ever leaving the institution—they typically felt vulnerable and frightened on every level. Although at the time it may seem the right thing to do for all involved, the decision to move into a new life pattern will undoubtedly be a hard time for all of us.

We have options. In some areas, there are social service programs coordinating these living arrangements. But if I do have to leave, I've made a pledge to myself that when the time comes to live in a facility for the aging, I will have already prepared to leave my home in gentle stages.

Author Mary C. Morrison describes moving from one's home as "a real wrench" that "brings another of the gifts of old age, the chance to say goodbye—a long, deep, fully conscious farewell." I will slowly and carefully give away my possessions as the time approaches. I will do a leave-taking ceremony, in which I go through my home saying goodbye to each room; perhaps I'll say a prayer or remove a small memento from each room as I go. It doesn't have to be extremely sad. It's so much better to grieve the loss and get on with it than not have the time to say goodbye.

I will not plunge into a serious depression or become anxious. I tell myself that these days, there are many resources for providing retirement community residents with wonderful opportunities for art, exercise, community work, and socializing, in addition to good medical care. Some facilities even offer field trips, fitness instructors, dancing, painting and cooking classes, gardening, and bridge. I cheer myself with the fact that in the 1950s, the average age of persons entering nursing homes was sixty-five, while now the age of admission is closer to eighty-five. So you and I have some time to plan and get used to the idea!

What will you do to make the transition easier for yourself when the time comes?

11
our families

The family is a school of compassion because it is here that we learn to live with other people.

—KAREN ARMSTRONG

As we age, our families become helpful and supportive, or neglectful and critical—they either value us or they don't. How they treat us is often a reflection of how we see ourselves. If we don't see ourselves as worthwhile contributors to society and we don't approach our aging with dignity and respect for ourselves, how can we expect them to see us that way?

I had lunch with my forty-year-old daughter recently, and she spent half the time talking about how society needs to readjust its attitudes toward its aging population. She reassured me that I would always be a valuable person in her life and that she would care for me, no questions asked, when I was older. I was grateful for her affirmation of our relationship and, at the same time, concerned that I would become a burden to her and her family. She reminded me that my attitude needed an adjustment, that I shouldn't see myself as becoming a burden to her or anyone else.

While I was writing this, my husband called from his office to say that his son from a previous marriage, Jacob, had just been hospitalized because of concerns about his heart. His call caused me to evaluate our role in the parenting of older children, and I'm thinking about how important our families are to us. How much we rely on each other for guidance, support, and security. How, as we age, our children are aging with us.

Our greater longevity has brought fundamental changes to our lives, and we are hardly aware of them, or maybe we take them for granted. In 1920, for example, ten-year-olds in the United States had only a 40 percent chance of having at least two of their grandparents alive. These days, that figure is 80 percent.

Our families have an effect on how we age, but our aging also has an effect on them. We can choose to inspire or instill fear. Joan Chittister wrote, "Our spiritual obligation is to age well—so that others who meet us may have the courage, the spiritual depth, to do the same."

AN EASY-TO-VISIT ELDER

I've decided to be an easy-to-visit elder
    to consider my effect on those
    who come by to see me
    to engage in their lives and mine
I'll plan for them to need me
    and not have a desperate need for them
I will not put my Ancient Mariner
    stranglehold on them
    with my tales of tiresome sorrows
Instead we'll exchange wisdom for energy
Exchange a story for some news
Eat homemade cakes
Drink fresh ground coffee
I want to be loved by younger people
    to have an open heart
    an easy laugh

an infectious appreciation of every moment
I will douse my fiery moral judgments
with the water of enthusiasm and wisdom
I will offer them a haven filled with peace and perspective,
    ask what they think and
    really listen

—P. D. BLAIR

Many of the younger generation complain that their elders (relatives or not) are tedious to visit. Perhaps we are because we haven't considered our effect on their time with us. We bore them because we haven't kept up with the world or we're too focused on our physical ailments. If we want the young to enjoy being with us, all we really have to do is be there for them, and they will visit as often as they can.

Think back to when you were younger. In your journal, describe an older woman you enjoyed visiting and what made it special.

MOVING TO THE CIRCUMFERENCE

I personally prefer to speak of this stage of adult development as a journey, a movement toward a new, unknown destination.

—JOYCE RUPP

At this stage, it may feel right and good to step down as family leader and decision maker. We can then wait on the periphery of family life and lean gently into it, aware of its promises and possibilities. Imagine life as a series of circles, growing wider and wider, spinning us to the outer edge, where eventually life feels satisfying and you pass the baton to the next generation.

The holidays are a time when you may sense that movement toward the circumference, where we are still part of the family circle but are no longer in the center. Take Thanksgiving, for example. I envision a day in the not-too-distant future when my house will no longer be the destination for everyone. There's a part of me that resists that inevitability and a part of me that is more than willing to give up the job of basting the turkey all day.

We've spent the best years of our lives multitasking the complicated managerial duties that family life requires to a point that they have become second nature to us. How can we possibly let them go? Sooner or later, we must do so, and the goal is to do so as gracefully as possible.

Imagine you are at the circumference. What would a holiday or other family gathering look like from that new perspective?

NEW GRANDMA

If your baby is "beautiful and perfect, never cries or fusses, sleeps on schedule and burps on demand, an angel all the time," you're the grandma.

—Teresa Bloomingdale

To fully experience the special event of your first grandchild, you might want to plan to be there for the delivery if the parents agree. Find out the hospital rules from the doctor who'll be performing the delivery. Sometimes grandparents are allowed in the delivery room, especially if it's their own daughter, perhaps in the background to respect the mother's modesty. If you can't witness the birth, you can be in the waiting room. Then you can hold the newborn and present your new grandchild with her first teddy bear and thank the new parents for the gift of a grandchild. If it's impossible to be at the birth or in the hospital while it's happening, try to make a trip to see the infant, and the parents, as soon as you can.

Don't be disappointed if the new parents don't want anyone—even grandparents—in the hospital at all. If that's the case, let the parents-to-be decide how to keep you posted. Coordinate your plans with those of the other grandparents to avoid any conflicts. Discuss the visit with the parents-to-be so you'll be able to comply with their wishes. A grandchild's birth can bring a distant family together, and with you on the scene to welcome the baby, the occasion can become a family celebration.

Ask the parents what they need. Chances are, they will have their hands very, very full, and your presence can be a great help to them. Grandparents, as visitors or surrogates, must learn to take their clues from the parents in order not to undermine their authority.

The new parents may not have planned anything to eat for their return home. If that's the case, why not bring in something special for the happy couple so they'll have meals for several days? Grandparents can help in countless ways, from basic housekeeping to giving the new mom time off for a nap. If there's no live-in housekeeper, one grandparent may actually move in for a while to ease the burden.

Is there anything about this new role that you might be uncomfortable with? In what way could you feel most useful during this time?

GRANDMOTHERING 101
(Even If You Have No Grandchildren of Your Own)

A grandmother is a lady who has no little children of her own. She likes other people's.

—ANONYMOUS GIRL, AGE 8

We don't necessarily have to give birth to a child to leave a legacy. My grandmother worked as a nanny and housekeeper for several families. At her funeral, the children she cared for, then in their fifties and sixties, lined up to pay their respects to her and to tell us the kind of positive, nurturing effect she'd had on their lives.

The role of grandparent has a way of splitting your personality into two opposing halves. One half of you believes in the traditional grandparent—the soft, warm, dependable, always-there kind; the other half is living energetically in the present, enjoying the freedoms that are finally possible. Today's grandmothers love their children and grandchildren, and most will do anything in the world for them, yet they refuse to follow the typical script and live at their beck and call.

Most grandmothers play an interested, active role in their grandchildren's lives. Despite busy lives and geographic separation, grandmothers can enjoy a strong closeness between the generations. Some even spend time with their grandchildren every day and are regular caregivers. They see their role as a companion or confidant. They give advice and share stories from the good old days. When visiting, they enjoy eating together, watching TV programs, shopping for clothes, playing sports, and attending church.

Remember that it's not too late to be a better grandmother than you were a mother. The birth and growth of grandchildren offer tremendous possibilities for repair and enrichment between the two older generations. Your children may ask for your advice in ways they never did at seventeen.

Here are some ideas and actions to keep in mind as you learn the grandmothering role:

- Learn to get along with, or cope with, the other grandparents who want time with the children also.

- Be sensitive to the values and disciplinary rules that the parents have for your grandchildren.

- Let the parents know that you have no desire to turn yourself into their on-call babysitter. (The irritation you feel when adult children take your time for granted can grow into seething resentment.)

In what ways would you like to be involved in the lives of your grandchildren (or other small children)?

DISTANCE GRANDPARENTING

Knowing how to be a grandmother does not come instinctively, any more than knowing how to be a mother simply flows in a woman's blood.

—Sheila Kitzinger

Your grandchildren may look to you for unconditional love and comfort when they are younger, and staying close to them can make it possible for you to help them through difficult times as they get older. It's important to stay in touch when grandchildren become teenagers. They often need someone other than friends to talk to. Keep a grandchild's confidence unless you feel his parents must know.

My good friend Ginena Dulley Wills said, "One of my greatest pleasures in midlife and beyond continues to be my family. I have found that keeping in touch with four grandsons in distant places takes energy and intentionality on the part of each of us."

I asked Ginena to contribute to this essay by offering advice to other grandmothers living a distance away from their grandkids. To my delight, she came up with this advice based on her experiences:

- Mail: I keep my letters short and simple, especially for the younger ones. They don't have the patience to listen to long letters. When on vacation or traveling, I send postcards, pictures, and brochures of where we have been. I often see them on the front of the fridge when I go to visit. Because one family lives in the South, it is fun to send dried leaves for the grandchildren to look at. Sometimes I include a stick of gum or a fridge magnet along with the letter.

- Phone: I try to be sensitive to the family routine so they are more likely to be available when I call. Younger children don't always respond while on the telephone, but they are probably smiling and nodding their heads as they enjoy listening. I try to keep abreast of what is happening in the lives of grandchildren so that I can call shortly before or after an event to share their excitement.

- Video chat and email: I enjoy keeping in touch with my grandchildren through their drawings. My son will sometimes scan and email homework or a drawing that one of the grandchildren has created. That way, they can keep the original and I still get to see it. We frequently exchange pictures and news on Facebook.

- Video: Video cameras and smartphone cameras have added a new dimension to keeping in touch on a frequent basis. It is great to be able to see special events as well as what they are doing in their everyday lives.

- I find it is so important to visit my children and grandchildren on a regular basis. Making the time to celebrate a special birthday, program at school, or special event in life is what keeps us close and connected to each other—you will never regret it.

I think Ginena's ideas are great. Here are a few of my own:

- Send them bedtime stories on audio or videotape, perhaps a chapter at a time.

- Share a movie or book you enjoyed or you think they might enjoy. After you've watched it or read it, send it through the mail, then talk about it during one of your scheduled phone calls.

- Start a separate travel savings fund to bring them to you, or you to them.

In your journal, write about what you would be willing to do to stay in touch with your grandchildren.

CAREGIVING GRANDCHILDREN

Grandma always made you feel she had been waiting to see just you all day and now the day was complete.

—MARCY DEMAREE

If you're caregiving a grandchild, it can be an enormously rewarding experience. I loved caring for my grandson after school. His 3:15 p.m. arrival offered a welcome break in my day and a chance to activate my own inner child—milk and cookies, homework help, and an occasional game of gin rummy. Research shows when older people care for others, their mental health improves, and even being matched with surrogate grandchildren has been shown to reduce depression and stress.

On the other hand, too much caregiving can have the opposite effect! When grandparents become the primary caregivers for their grandchildren, some studies suggest that those grandparents are twice as likely to be depressed as non-caregiving grandparents. The researchers postulate that it might be the exhaustion, isolation, and financial and physical stress (especially caring for toddlers). This sounds similar to what I experienced when I was a young mother. Who doesn't want to run away from home and responsibility during those exhausting years and check themselves into a locked ward?

For a variety of reasons, some grandmothers are caring for a grandchild full-time. In these cases, it's important to not go it alone. There are about four hundred to five hundred grandparent caregiver support groups around the country as well as respite programs so Grandma can take the weekend off. Try the grandparent resources provided by AARP, or start a support group for grandmas in your community.

If you don't have grandchildren, or if yours that don't live nearby, in what ways can you can share your gifts with a younger child in your community?

CAREGIVING OUR PARENTS

In the past year, I lost my mother to cancer and helped my father move to a retirement home. . . . I learned that I can manage more than I thought I could!

—SALLY, AGE 55

Thanks to modern medicine, the older population continues to grow, and women, who have become the default caregivers of our society, could end up caring for their parents for many years of their lives.

Here are some suggestions for managing the caregiving:

- Consult a geriatrician, a doctor who specializes in seniors and is tuned in to quality-of-life issues, especially if the primary care doctor doesn't seem to be adequately addressing your parent's concerns.

- Depression is a prevalent problem among the very old and is widely underrecognized and undertreated, so familiarize yourself with the signs.

- Know the details about what treatment your parents would want should they become unable to make decisions. This may entail establishing a living will, health care proxy, or health care power of attorney.

- If your parents want to stay in their own community, find out about the resources available there.

- Guilt can become mingled with resentment and rage. We think, *How much of my life am I supposed to give up to do this?* If you are asking this question, perhaps the burden of care is not equally distributed among your family members.

- Be ready to compromise, delegate responsibilities, and ask for help whenever possible so you don't neglect your own physical, emotional, and mental health.

- Set boundaries; try to see your time together as a gift and a way of deepening your relationship.

While caring for an elderly parent, we can learn many coping skills from them. If someone has made it to eighty or ninety years old, they've done something right, and you might learn something valuable from them. Sit down for an hour, reminisce about old times, or page through an old photo album together. If you see caregiving a parent as a burden, it will become one. On the other hand, if you see it as a learning experience and a challenge, you will feel rewarded and proud of yourself each time you resolve a conflict or a problem.

Now it's time for you. Make a list of actions you could take that would nourish your body, mind, and spirit. Write one action on your calendar every day, and do it. Listen to music, sit in a chapel, or take a walk. Gather information on diet, exercise, and stress reduction. Confide in someone like a nonjudgmental sibling, therapist, close friend, or neighbor. Find a support group for caregivers.

If you are caregiving a parent, what actions can you take that would benefit your parent? What actions can you take that would benefit you?

PARENTING ADULT CHILDREN

Denial is believing that your adult children and their spouses will appreciate your setting them straight on everything from where they should live to what they should eat.

—"Judge Judy" Sheindlin

If you have children, they are likely somewhere between the ages of twenty-five and fifty. The questions remain: What is our role as parents of our grown children? How do we parent and relate to these old kids? What do we do when the kids hit us up for a loan, or move back home . . . or use our homes for storage? How do we react when they want to butt into our business?

A friend of mine said, "First of all, stay away from your adult children as much as possible. They not only make you look older, but they can actually make you feel older." I say, if staying away from your "old" children is not possible or would be unkind, consider buying them a facelift! Well, it's not possible to stay away from them forever, so we need to learn to live among them on the same planet.

Author Florida Scott-Maxwell wrote, "No matter how old a mother is she watches her middle-aged children for signs of improvement." This couldn't be more true for me. Not only do I watch for signs of improvement in my children, but I also sometimes find myself wanting to live their lives so I can change the outcome to an easier one for me to look at! As my forty-year-old daughter Aimee reminds me, "Mom, you bother me sometimes. You worry about me too much. Just listen when I talk, and stop trying to fix things, so I can feel free to learn and mature from my own trials and errors."

Is your urge to meddle in your adult children's lives so overwhelming that you just can't help yourself? I can't tell you how many times I've slipped back into treating my adult children like they're eight years old. "Wear your jacket. It's cold outside," or "Are you eating enough vegetables?" It's hard to let go of the mother role and to see your children as adults.

Some young adults take a very long time and follow a very circuitous route before they eventually find their way in the world. Financial pressures and divorces are most likely to send adult children back to the nest. Close to 20 million young adults live with their parents, and that doesn't account for all those who have boomeranged back more than once. Jean, age fifty-nine, said, "I waved goodbye to my youngest offspring, squaring my shoulders and gritting my teeth as I turned to do battle with the empty-nest demons. Three months later, he was back!" A goodly percentage of kids ages twenty-five to thirty-four are still living in their family homes, and some never left. Some boomerang kids may rotate in and out for years, if not decades, constantly changing the household's dynamics.

If your son or daughter shows up on your doorstep, you will need a clear plan regarding rent and other financial contributions, chores, house rules about visitors and smoking, and any other expectations you have. Keep a united front with your spouse so your child doesn't pit one of you against the other. Set a limit on how long he can stay. Encourage your child to move on with his life and to create a well-defined plan. If the child has a drug problem, deal with it right away. Any kindness you offer should be conditional upon his enrollment in a treatment program.

Adult children still crave our approval, and we must not judge their behavior in the same way we did when they were young. Our corrections and suggestions can have a negative emotional impact. When parents and adult children live far apart, their brief visits can turn into replays of child-parent relationships that might turn explosive.

Our kids aren't kids anymore. They're over twenty-one, and they're supposed to behave like adults, and when they don't, it's hard to hold your tongue. When your children are married and you see things they or their spouses are doing that you don't approve of, keep it to yourself—even if you think it was your faulty parenting that created the hardship.

If you're a parent, you know that guilt is a constant companion. It's not surprising that a generation like ours, which prides itself on self-reflection, ends up blaming itself for our children's failure to thrive in the world. It's crucial that we stop thinking like that. The key to our sanity and survival, as well as theirs, is detachment—not from our children but from their problems. We must acknowledge the limits of our parental responsibility and accept that we have done as much as we possibly could for them.

How can you continue to be a part of your children's lives in a healthy, balanced way?

CHANGING PLACES: MOVING IN WITH YOUR KIDS

Inside every older person there's a younger person wondering what happened.

—Ashleigh Brilliant

Uncomfortable emotions click into place when I consider living with my children someday. Suppose I move in with them and act like a teenager—that would teach them a lesson, wouldn't it?

On a serious note, I feel that most of us put the option of living with our children at the bottom of the list of choices for living out our old age. I can imagine that for some of you, it would be a joy to be around grandchildren, to feel useful in some way, and to be part of a family once again. But since I like some measure of control over my environment and a lot of peace and quiet, it would make me miserable unless I had a completely separate apartment connected to their house or a small bungalow on their property.

My daughter has already announced that she will never put me in a nursing home to be neglected or abused, as she puts it. Yet if I am ill and need care, I see moving in with her and her family as one big pain in the ass for all of them and me as well. Do I want to end my life being a pain in the ass to someone?

Author M. F. K. Fisher has this beautiful thought: "Children and old people and the parents in between should be able to live together, in order to learn how to die with grace, together." I suppose she's right. Dying surrounded by family wouldn't be the hard part for me. The hard part would be living with them and feeling I was in the way. I guess I'll need to wait until the time comes and decide then what's in the best interest of us all.

Under what circumstances and guidelines would you be willing to live with your adult children?

ROBOTIC ROMEO

The trick for younger family members is to help without feeling trapped and overwhelmed; the trick for older members is to accept help while preserving dignity and control.

—MARY PIPHER

I have a habit of stacking up magazines and letting them marinate for a year or two until I get good and ready to read them. Then, like a hungry wood fire, I burn through them, slashing and hacking away at ads and peripherals (like those annoying subscription cards and perfume samples) until I have only a stack of articles left. On a recent foray into my magazine stash, I came across an article in an issue of *Scientific American*. It seems some company has created a robot to serve as a companion and helper for the elderly. It's a robot called the HelpMate. It has arms, voice recognition, and stereo vision.

I began to imagine my life with one of these things. There I am missing my grandkids or my husband, and my HelpMate responds to my tear-inflected pleas. I tell his voice-recognition chip that I'm lonely, and he embraces me in his steely arms, gazing at me with the kind blue stereo-vision marbles he has for eyes. He feels cold. His little robot face presses against mine. My tears short-circuit his whirring electronics. Brrrrrrr. Cold.

I worry that my kids and friends will think the little robot a substitute for visits with me. I imagine them taking him off in a corner one Sunday afternoon and telling him, "Make sure she doesn't sleep past ten a.m., and get her to take her red pills before lunch and the green-and-white one with dinner." Oh God. Could this be my future? "And when she starts to reminisce about the old days, sit quietly without comment, nodding until she's done. Don't forget to look interested." Cold. "Oh, and when she complains about her children and how we never come to see her, tell her it was just yesterday they were here—she'll never know the difference; she loses track of the days anyway." A frosty future with a robotic HelpMate complete with empathic listening, steely arms, stereo vision, and programmed compassionate responses. Ugh.

I have a plan. If presented with this robotic sorry excuse for a companion, I will take my elderly self and the steely little guy on a shopping trip. I will dress him up in a dark, long-haired wig, a white silk shirt, and a tuxedo. Then I will take him for a tour of the Hawaiian Islands and spend every cent of my children's inheritance on hula lessons!

How do you feel about the possibility of this technological advance?

UNFINISHED FAMILY BUSINESS

We have a choice about whether we forgive others including our parents and heal ourselves or let the hurts go on festering.

—Betty Nickerson

An older friend of mine has not spoken to her parents or siblings since she graduated high school. I have other friends who are very close to severing family ties because they get continuing aggravation instead of the understanding and support they want. Leaving these issues unresolved can keep you stuck in the energy of the past forever, and going forward in your life, you're going to need all the energy you can muster.

Acknowledging your anger and disappointment with family members is key to moving into a healing process with them. Many years ago, my therapist helped me honor my anger at my father, to make meaning of it all, and ultimately to move toward forgiveness. Allowing room for anger let me move to a place where forgiveness and understanding could be born.

What does it mean to forgive? *Webster's* defines it as "to give up resentment against or the desire to punish; stop being angry with; to give up all claim to punish or exact penalty." If we are to forgive, we must first surrender the right to get even. We then cease defining the one who hurt us in terms of the hurt that was caused. There is nothing in this definition about approving of the injurer's actions. If we forgive, we can also reach a point where we wish our injurers well—after we've worked on making meaning of the situation, this act then becomes some kind of miracle.

Letting go of negative feelings toward others is highly dependent on our ability to let go of negative feelings toward ourselves. When we have developed the ability to let go of our own past mistakes, to acknowledge our humanness, it's amazing how effortless it becomes to let go of the mistakes of others.

If family members can't give you the support you need in an area that is sensitive to you, try to find some aspect of your life you can comfortably share with them. In some cases where a bridge can't be built, you may have to create what becomes a new family. It's never too late to do so. Weathering the storms of life isn't easy, and loving relationships can be a lifeboat—a lifeboat you can build by choosing new family members.

I enlisted a new family for myself when I realized mine wasn't capable of giving me all of what I needed. When I was developing my new family, I never directly asked anyone to fill the roles. I learned about each person's background and developed a plan to strengthen the relationship. I invited each one into my life, eventually sharing intimate details. Author Roberta Russell describes how she re-created a family after losing her family to divorces and death. "I carefully chose six people for my new family. One was a great teacher . . . another, an excellent father . . . and so on."

No family connection of any kind would last if the silent reparative force of forgiveness were not working almost constantly to counteract the corrosive effects of resentment and bitterness. The wish to repair a wounded relationship, whether it takes the form of forgiveness, apology, or some other bridging gesture, is a basic human impulse. Forgiveness is not just a by-product of growth: the struggle to forgive can promote growth, and that is my point. We are meant to keep growing as long as we live.

What unfinished family business is draining your energy? And what are you willing to do about it?

CREATING A FAMILY HISTORY

*As an older family member, you give your family a sense of
heritage, tradition and continuity that only your generation
can provide.*

—Eudora Seyfer

There comes a point in our lives when we'd like to pass on at least a portion of our family history to the next generation. At my grandmother's one hundredth birthday party, my son, then ten years old, interviewed her on videotape, asking about her voyage from Sweden to the United States in 1913. This taped interview is of course a precious historic record of immense importance to my family. Although Grandma Agda was somewhat fuzzy about the details of her earlier life, and the videotaping process wore her out a bit, she seemed grateful for the opportunity to pass on this part of her history.

We naturally want some of our life story to live beyond us, to put our own lives into a historical perspective. The Internet offers a treasure trove of genealogical information like directories of surnames, adoption and birth records, cemetery and marriage records, military records, ships' passenger lists, census records, immigration records, and a lot more. You can even find family sites that offer family trees, wills, and photographs.

You can write out your story and pass it on. You can give your family and friends a portrait of how you see yourself and what you have brought to your family and the world. Try making an uncritical list of remembered experiences and life events. Write down as many details as you can about the memories. It may not be easy, but be honest—you need not share all details, but tell the truth about what you do choose to write. Writing this kind of honest memoir usually generates a sense of well-being, and that can lead to new insights about one's life and an emotional resolution to some troublesome problems.

Do you know where you fit in your family's history? What stories would you like to preserve for your descendants?

12
our friends

This third act—from age fifty on—can be the best act. If people know that you see them . . . that you hear them, that you really are taking them in, then you will never be without friends.

—NANCY FRIDAY

My good friends enrich my life. They make the good times better and the bad times bearable. They give me support and help me stay connected to what's important. They help energize me and reduce my stress. The preciousness of life matters more to me now, and good, intimate friends matter more now than the superficial ones of my earlier years.

We need to increase our human contacts for a longer and less stressful life. Close relationships at home, on the job, and in the community can keep you calm and help boost your immune system. It's important to make regular connections with people you like, to stay in touch with old friends, and to attend meetings of community groups—to make connections part of your everyday life.

When I get busy with my work and my family, my tendency is to let my friendships slide. That's really a mistake because women can be such a source of strength for each other. We intuitively find it easy to nurture one another. We need to create unpressured space where we can engage in the special kind of talk that women do when they're with other women.

The famed Nurses' Health Study from Harvard Medical School found that the more friends women had, the less likely they were to develop physical impairments as they aged and the more likely they were to be leading a joyful life. In fact, the results were so significant, the researchers concluded that not having close friends or confidants was as detrimental to women's health as smoking or being overweight. When they looked at how well the women functioned after the death of their spouses, they found that even in the face of this biggest stressor of all, those women who had a close friend and confidant were more likely to survive the experience without any new physical impairment or permanent loss of vitality.

The issues and concerns about aging point to the necessity of creating and maintaining support systems, the ability to make new friends as old ones die, the need to strengthen existing relationships, and the call to be involved in community affairs. Friendship is one of life's most special gifts. I encourage you to look at the value of friends and the support they offer as you age and how the quality of your friendships can affect your health and longevity.

WHAT MATTERS

I like being with women who have discovered the joy of who they are, who know that what matters more than age is whether or not they are strengthening their creative spirits, living authentic lives.

—GAIL BALDEN

Does it matter that you have one more gray hair today, or that you have one more day on the planet to connect with those around you? Does it matter that you have arthritis in your elbows and arms, or that you have arms in which to hold a friend who needs a shoulder to cry on? Does it matter that you can't remember the things you used to, or that you remember how loved you've felt in your life?

What matters changes as we move into the second half of our lives. Giving back seems to matter more now. Author Shirley Mitchell wrote, "After 50, we find the joy of giving back, of pouring into others, of returning and serving out of the rich storehouse of the knowledge and experience we have gained." I couldn't agree more.

You may be the most important person in someone's life today. Have you considered how even the smallest gesture of friendship can change the course of a life? Consider the enormity of this truth. Isn't what matters most, as you view your life from its second half, how much you've expanded your capacity for love?

Today, are you willing to let a special friend know how much he or she matters to you?

THE COMPANY OF OTHER WOMEN

I find myself learning from women in their twenties, and from friends in their seventies. Perhaps the most important gift of the feminine life cycle is the gift of one another.

—JOAN BORYSENKO

Our women friends are there at the births of our ideas and our children; they are there for the high points we celebrate, the losses we endure, and the deaths we journey to and through. Author Janet Quinn says, "We are not passive observers of each other's lives; we help each other live them. Women friends. Womanfriend. I cannot imagine my life without them."

I don't know what would become of me if it weren't for the company of other women in my life. Women who are older offer me glimpses of what life can be in later years. Younger women offer an opportunity to share some of my hard-won wisdom and keep me in the swing of things. Most importantly, the women who are in my age group, who are moving through the journey with me, are my comforters, my jovial companions, and my confidants.

Those who have strong social connections are healthier and live longer than those who lack them. In particular, having a special friend and confidant is especially beneficial. Some studies found that socially involved people are less subject to depression and better able to handle stress, and get this—they're even less susceptible to the common cold!

When I was up against some of the hardest times in my life, my friends reminded me I would survive, as I had so many times before. They listened to my truth and mirrored back for me who I was when I had forgotten. That's the joy of women's friendships. We hold one another up when we're down. We listen with our hearts. We are honest with each other, and we remind each other about our goodness and strength. We join in each other's grief and loss. And perhaps most important of all, we know how to have fun when we're together. Betty-Clare Moffatt wrote this wish for her future: "When I am an old woman, I shall laugh hysterically with other old women, as we help each other across the street."

Sometimes the best thing friends can do is be loyal and understanding enough that you don't need to see them or call them or remind them you love them. Sometimes you just need friends to understand that you need to be alone. Growing old, really old, is part of life, and we must support and nurture each other the best we can.

In your journal, write about a particularly heartwarming experience you have had in the company of other women.

COMPANIONS ON THE JOURNEY

The thing about old friends is not that they love you, but that they know you. . . . They look at you and don't really think you look older because they've grown old along with you.

—ANNA QUINDLEN

I think growing older with friends is fun. Their companionship is especially valuable when they join you in lightening up about the whole process. My friend Sari and I joke about having surgery to move the soft pads on our hip bones up to our shoulders to use as shoulder pads. My sister Marilyn and I joke all the time about how our old-age spots are one day going to connect to each other and give us the look of a year-round tan!

Good friends are such an asset, I can't imagine a life without them. Author Patricia Lynn Reilly says, "Imagine a woman who values the women in her life. A woman who sits in circles of women. Who is reminded of the truth about herself when she forgets." We do forget from time to time who we really are and what it is we bring into this world. Friends who know us well and who are supportive by nature have no trouble reminding us of our value when we're down and out.

In the early to middle part of the 1900s, women weren't generally considered as interesting company as men. Barbara Sher implies that an interesting shift took place in the 1960s: "We woke up, looked around and discovered a world full of fascinating women. Why didn't we see them before?" Well, I'm seeing them now and appreciating them even more than I could have possibly imagined.

Write about your three most important female companions and why they are important to your journey.

MAKING NEW FRIENDS AND CLEANING OUT THE OLD

I have never had so many friends. They are not only interesting and stimulating, they are generous and uncritical. Most of them are women.

—Rebecca Latimer

A good friend is honest without being cruel. She is reliable, keeps her promises, and offers support when you need it. A real friend is not judgmental, is a good listener, and is someone you can have fun with.

Some friendships actually drain your energy and erode your self-esteem. Some so-called friends have upset, disappointed, or betrayed you. It's never too late to let go of these unhelpful relationships. Why do we make and maintain such friendships? For one thing, no one comes into our lives bearing a label that says *promise breaker* or *fault finder*. It can take time for a friendship to reveal itself as good or bad. We may hold on to a toxic friendship because we believe we won't at our age be able to make new ones.

Forming new friendships is key to healthy aging, and women with close, nontoxic friends live longer than those who lack them. For example, supportive friendships can improve your chances with cancer. A recent study of ovarian cancer patients indicated that women with strong social support have lower levels of a factor that stimulates tumor growth. Solid, supportive relationships relieve stress, lowering blood levels of stress hormones. Friends who truly care about you are more likely to cajole you into seeking medical help and to take care of you when you need it. Centenarians report that they have a remarkable network of nontoxic friends who care about them and offer help when needed.

It might be helpful to rekindle old friendships from your childhood and young adult years. Having these people as part of your life in later years is sure to prove meaningful. Next time you're invited to a class, workplace, sporting event, or other reunion, make it a point to attend and renew friendships or make a new friend.

To turn an acquaintance into a friend, you need to take a risk or two. Let her see you as you really are. Share something of yourself that you would not share with just anybody. Suggest spontaneous activities to do together. Listen to what matters to her. Ask for advice or for help on a project. Tell her you like her. If you sense an issue, bring up the situation and work it out together.

Sometimes our own comfort can be found in giving comfort to others, and as a bonus, a giving spirit increases longevity. You boost the spirit of someone in a touchy situation, and you get to live longer!

Think about your five closest friendships. Do these relationships uplift you or drain you?

WHEN FRIENDS DIE

When pain and fatigue wrestle, fatigue wins. The eye shuts. Then the pain rises again at dawn. At first you can stare at it, then it blinds you.

—Marge Piercy

I lost a precious friend this year. Anne Dean, I think of you often and how much of a gift it was to be caring for you as you fought against death.

There's no easy way to deal with the inevitability of losing friends. If you live long enough, friends are going to die. You may even live long enough to have all your friends die before you do. One of the best ways to deal with the loss is in a creative way. My sister dealt with the loss of one of her friends by writing this poem:

Liz

. . . Liz, I think of you . . . , especially
when trees are bare, December's empty arms
praising the sky . . .
I want to think of how things grow, not how they die
I want to remember the Magic Pan where you and I
would sit for hours, laughing, planning, scheming
about the usual stuff, hopes high
So, Liz,
I promise you, yeah, I really mean it, I've had enough . . .
when Spring comes again, and everything is fresh
I'm really gonna try
to lose the sadness.

—Marilyn Houston

You will never forget those friends who've gone before you, and with time, other friends will come to touch your life. And in the meantime, remember, if you've lost a friend, you now have a personal guardian angel watching over you.

Is there a creative way you can remember a friend who has passed?

WHERE IS EVERYBODY?

I was looking at my address book. Just about everybody in it is dead! I was thinking of putting together a new address book, but I didn't like the idea of leaving all those folks' names out.

—SARAH L. DELANY

When we were younger, death seemed distant and somehow impersonal. But gradually, or suddenly, as we age, more people around us die. They don't all die. Some just move away and retire in another state or another country, like my friend Maxine who moved to New Zealand.

We are older and so are our friends and relatives. Death becomes relevant, personal, close. Lives once unshakable are shaken by death or by loss—the loss of dreams, the loss of friends, the loss of relationships, the loss of health, or the loss of the ability to function.

What do we do? In addition to the old friends you've acquired, consider making some younger ones. Having younger friends will keep you more engaged with new ideas and more physically active while also helping you to maintain a younger attitude and lifestyle for yourself.

Betty Friedan wrote, "Most of my friends are younger. . . . You need to make friends that are younger. I have to say that in the last couple of years, three of the men in my life have died, and the women are still going strong."

What qualities would you like a new friend to have?

CLASS REUNIONS

When I went to my fortieth reunion, I couldn't help but ask my-self, who are those old people?

—CAROL, AGE 59

I think women spend more energy on crash diets and fixing themselves up for a class reunion than for any other major event in their lives besides their own wedding. What are we trying to prove? That we haven't aged a bit? Are we still trying to get back at the guy who ignored us all through high school? You know, the one you had a crush on so bad you thought you couldn't live another day without him? Or that skinny blond cheerleader who bullied you?

Despite swearing I would never ever do it, I went to the thirtieth reunion of my high school class. I hadn't seen most of those "kids" since I graduated. None of my old friends looked great, although of course I think I did. I dropped twenty pounds in preparation and made sure I wore my best jewelry. The same cliques were operating at the reunion. Those friends who were tight then were still huddling close together, eying and assessing the other attendees.

I remember the days when we wore strange clothes and listened to music that made our parents crazy. We trusted no one over thirty and shocked our parents by rejecting the accepted Establishment values. We were passionate and idealistic. By our sheer numbers, we defined our times. That was more than forty years ago, and the baby boomer generation has officially reached a ripe age. The idealism of youth has been exchanged for concerns over health care costs. As opposed to then, our drug of choice is now a potent over-the-counter pain medication. Now we hardly trust anyone under the age of thirty, especially young doctors! And hey, man, when did we become the Establishment?

If you went to your high school reunion, what issues did it bring up for you? If you didn't, what issues did you imagine would come up if you had attended?

THE YEAH-YEAH SISTERHOOD

Sometimes it only takes a word, a phrase, a drumbeat, a circle, a song, a room full of women in harmony together, to remind us of all that we are.

—BettyClare Moffatt

Once a year, I join a small group of women on an adventure like no other I ever experienced in my younger years. Sari and Patty rent a house on Plum Island off the Massachusetts coast, and each year, they create a space for five of us to join one another in a ritual of sisterhood. We design and make things that reflect our authentic nature. One year, we styled hats by using glue guns, bows, shells, and assorted other decorative items. When we posed for a photo wearing our hats, I realized just what a bonding experience we had created.

Another year, we made purses to wear with our hats. Again, out came the glue gun, feathers, beads, and shells. One of us in the sisterhood bought outlandish muumuus for each of us at a thrift store, and we posed once again as a group with our hats and purses as accessories.

One of us, Julie, described her experience as follows: "I am the youngest of this group of extraordinary women. As I look at each of these women, it's like looking into a window of what may or may not happen to me when I reach their stage in life. I've been given a rare insight to my future. We all have very different careers, marital status, upbringing, size—and yet I feel such unity as a group. We learn so many things from one another. Because of them, I look forward to new journeys of age with whatever time I have left on the planet."

Write about an idea for creating a bonding experience for a group of women that you know.

13
our play

No matter how old we are, we are still that little girl that skipped rope, roller-skated on the sidewalk, skinned knees, wore braids with barrettes or ribbons, and ate ice cream.

—Jo Schlehofer

As we grow older, must we grow more serious? Do we need to stop being playful and young spirited? Ask yourself, *What gives me pleasure and delight?* Have you forgotten? Did you leave your inner child behind at the playground?

Your need to play doesn't diminish with age. No self-help book, Indian guru, or bossy sister can tell you what will give you pleasure. You have to divine it for yourself and listen for your inner child's urges.

Each day, I ask myself, *Have I done anything fun yet?* We need to laugh at ourselves more and get out and play. Someone once wrote, "If you laugh . . . you last!" That's true. I remember my grandmother who, at seventy-five, got down on the floor with us to shoot marbles and play hopscotch on the sidewalk out front. She made time for fun and lived to be 102!

I got an email a few days ago that said, "You don't stop laughing because you grow old, you grow old because you stop laughing." Wow, is that true. A sense of play and a sense of humor are essential to aging successfully.

I urge you to put more fun in your life, to develop a sense of humor, to seek adventure, to remain curious, and to take the needs of your inner child seriously.

ARE WE HAVING FUN YET?

If I'd known how much fun, what freedom, would be found in these September years, I would've lied about my age and gotten here sooner.

—LYNNE ZIELINSKI

The average number of times an adult laughs in a day is fifteen, and kids laugh 150 times a day. When was the last time you had some good, old-fashioned fun?

My grandmother skipped rope when she was in her sixties—just for fun. Remember skipping without a jump rope? Skipping burns almost as many calories as running, and it's more fun. I even read somewhere that you can join a skipping club!

If you aren't a naturally happy person, with very little effort you can cultivate pleasure. If you take having fun and creating pleasure seriously, you will find ways to reorient your inner compass and change your thoughts and feelings. With a little effort, you can shift your mood. Author Rebecca Latimer wrote, "Somewhere along the way I picked up the idea that if I refuse negative thoughts and emotions, if I smile rather than frown, laugh rather than cry, my mood changes entirely." I believe her.

I'm not talking about activities you could do in your sleep. And eating doesn't count unless you are truly immersed in the act of cooking, serving, and tasting. The pleasure in most rote activities, if there is any, wears off in about ten seconds. Rote activities don't get you to the state of sustained well-being I would call pleasure. Experiment with activities that require attention, like learning a language, painting a mural, or taking your grandchildren to the park. For instance, while I was on a trip to Hilton Head Island with some girlfriends in their sixties, we rented three-wheelers and rode around the island for a day joyriding like little kids. Lose yourself, forget about time, and come back feeling different.

One sixty-two-year-old woman I spoke to gets up at 6:15 a.m. to knit and listen to classical music before she starts a busy day of volunteer work. Another runs marathons on the weekends for the sheer exhilaration of it, and one eighty-two-year-old takes piano lessons for, as she puts it, "the high of it." Have fun just for the sake of having fun. Blow bubbles—the added benefit is that you inhale oxygen, which is good for the brain. Play with pipe cleaners or Play-Doh—it's also good for exercising arthritic hands. Draw with crayons, paint with watercolors, and by all means, get a glue gun and make something.

Write about things you've had fun doing in the past—could you do them now?

LAUGHING OUT LOUD

> *Zen practitioners . . . believe that laughing out loud is the only way to reconcile our wish to attain enlightenment with our repeated failure to do so.*
>
> —Véronique Vienne

Comedian Fred Allen warns: "It's bad to suppress laughter; it goes back down and spreads to your hips."

Could guffawing yourself silly actually be good for your health? It certainly can. In 1979, magazine editor Norman Cousins suggested that laughter was powerful medicine, and recent studies have proven him right. Frequent laughing, the harder the better, can lower blood pressure, increase protective antibodies, and even cut the risk of heart disease.

Daily laughter is a health elixir. There are about one hundred laughter clubs in the United States where members perform exercises at health centers, nursing homes, schools, and corporations. Look on the Internet to find a nearby laughter club.

Dr. Lee Berk, a pioneer of laughter research at Loma Linda University School of Medicine in California said, "We're taking laughing to the molecular level now. We're using the sophisticated tools of the twenty-first century to establish what the Bible told us centuries ago: 'A merry heart doeth good like a medicine.'"

Write about some things that are guaranteed to make you laugh, and do them.

A SENSE OF HUMOR

If you could choose one characteristic that would get you through life, choose a sense of humor.

—JENNIFER JONES

I remember my mother (then in her fifties) sitting next to me in my 1966 VW Beetle when we were caught in a downpour. As I started the car, Mom said hurriedly, "Are your windshield workers wiping?" When I repeated back to her what she said, we both burst into uncontrollable laughter.

Have you ever had trouble finding the word for a familiar object? The older I get, the more of a challenge it's become. I once told my husband I was putting the dirty dishes in the garage (it has a door and you put stuff in it!) instead of saying dishwasher. I still laugh when I think about it.

The *Journal of Personality and Social Psychology* reported that women who had the biggest smiles in their college yearbook photos had happier lives, happier marriages, and fewer personal setbacks in the following thirty years. (Go ahead, check your yearbook.)

Put on a happy face, and your body, either hoping for the best or not knowing the difference, responds as if the expression were genuine. Smiling engages at least three major muscle groups, increasing blood flow to the face and creating a rosy glow. Who couldn't use that? Laugh wholeheartedly, and your facial muscles will become toned; get delirious, and give yourself a serious aerobic workout that helps your immune system at the same time.

Even the gentlest smile causes your eyes to moisten. The muscles around the tear glands are stimulated, causing your eyes to sparkle and shine. Draw back your lips, and your raised cheeks round out your face, softening it; the increased blood flow nourishes your skin. Try finding lotions at the makeup counter that promise those results! And the next time you have trouble finding a word or name, laugh at yourself—you will end up looking much younger.

How can you put more smiles and laughter in your life?

CHALLENGES AND POSSIBILITIES

Challenges are gifts that force us to search for a new center of gravity. Don't fight them. Just find a new way to stand.

—OPRAH WINFREY

In your future and present, do you see possibility or disability? I don't believe we're all stimulated by the wit or the irony of life. Some of us are decked by it.

I wonder how many of us are so challenged by fear of the unknown that we've squeezed out a sense of joy and play in our lives—stimulated only by the desire to stay young, stay beautiful, stay alive.

We all know what our challenges are. For some, aging is a challenge in itself. A challenge to stay vital, healthy, and interested in life. Perhaps even in the face of challenge, we can be more proactive in seeking out the small adventures, life's sideshows. You know, the ones that aren't necessarily the main events.

Make a habit of driving or walking down a different street each day. Learn how to play the harmonica, or do like my friend Patty did—arrange for a tugboat ride. Add one small challenge, one adventure, into your life today.

How can you put a bit more fun and adventure into your life?

WONDER YEARS

The return of "wonder" in old age is illustrated in "elder tales" down through the ages . . . showing older people apparently outrageous or foolish after years of being practical and predictable.

—Betty Friedan

The way Betty Friedan describes wonder in the above quote makes it sound like a valuable pursuit for my later years. She also says that this wonder is "an essential element of wisdom." I agree.

Have you become predictable and boringly practical in your older years? Is it time to plan some wonder-filled events? Author Valerie Bell says, "Aging well takes some planning. It's so easy to lose focus, fail to stretch for the best life has to offer, and end life full of regrets."

Sit quietly for a period of time today, and think back to when you felt a sense of wonder at a particular event or time or place in your life. Then imagine yourself doing that activity. I remember when a sunrise took my breath away. We were on vacation in Cape Cod, and we drove the car to the beach at five a.m. We simply sat there listening to music in the car while we wondered at that gorgeous fiery ball rising from its sleep.

I'll run out to watch a sunset this week because I'm not going to wait for a vacation to do this wonder-filled activity. Five minutes from my Vermont home is Lake Champlain, where there is a beautiful park overlooking the lake with hills that slope gently to the water. At around seven p.m., I will sit on my folding chair atop one of those gentle slopes, drink wine, read poetry, and watch the sun set the horizon, and my soul, on fire.

In what ways can you exercise your sense of wonder and joy?

TRAVELING ADVENTURES

Here I am, eighty-three years old, and I have just returned from yet another travel of discovery to the Greek Islands.

—HELEN HAYES

You don't need to go all the way to Greece to expand your horizons—there is someplace new and interesting for you to explore within a day's bus ride or drive of your home. Even a short trip opens us to our need for new adventure, in purpose and project, a new exercise for our bodies and our spirit.

If your husband or partner doesn't want to join you or can't, consider what these adventurous women did. Joei Carlton Hossack, fifty-nine, has been traveling on her own in an RV. Her husband died of a heart attack when she was forty-eight, and she continued to travel on her own in their VW Westfalia. She's authored many books on solo travel. What an inspiration!

My sixty-five-year-old friend Ellen went alone to the Club Med resort in Sonora Bay in Mexico to participate in the big tennis camp they have there. And another sixty-eight-year-old friend, Barbara, took off on her own to see the United States in her ancient Volvo wagon.

Is a disability keeping you or your husband home? More adventures are available these days for the disabled. And recreation vehicles with disabled access are now available for purchase or rent with features like wheelchair lifts, wide entrances, roll-in showers, and so on.

If you were to have a traveling adventure, where would you go? What steps can you take today to make it happen?

JUICY CURIOSITY

If you have twenty years or more stretching out before you, now is the time to learn something new.

—RUTH TURK

Curiosity can still be an innocent exploration like it was when we were children. We can be newly refreshed by our world—we can see things with awe and wonder, with new eyes. The task is to become curiouser and curiouser. To look at the world afresh before we leave it. Maybe you won't be successful in staving off some physical challenges like arthritis, but there's no need to let your sense of curiousity grow rigid and inflexible.

Twelfth-century mystic Hildegard of Bingen counseled her devotees to be "juicy people." According to her teachings, to be juicy is to be a fearlessly joyous optimist, a troublemaker tirelessly afflicting the comfortable, a passionate lover of tasty food and good talk, "a frequent violator of the ordinance against indecent exposure of the heart, and a guerrilla in the insurrection against Dream Molesters everywhere." She wants us all to be filled with wonder and curiosity, with lusty appetites and high spirits, to embrace life, liberty, and the pursuit of happiness.

Make an effort to stay interested in life like Jeanne Calment, who lived to be 122 years old and said, "I think I will die laughing. . . . Everything interests me. I've had a fine life."

Stay curious; be juicy and inquisitive. Ask questions—when you go to a store that displays and sells pottery or art, ask how it was produced. Go to the library to research a topic you know little about. Buy an old telephone at a garage sale, and take it apart—haven't you always wondered how they work?

Find the answers to some things you've been curious about, and write in your journal what you've learned.

OUR INNER CHILD NEVER GROWS OLD

Because I was once a child, I am always a child. . . . My past is part of what makes the present Madeleine and must not be denied or rejected or forgotten.

—Madeleine L'Engle

I'm trying to learn to accept all my inner selves, the new and old, the child and the adult, not as strangers but as friends. Do you wonder if you have an inner child? Like Russian nested dolls, we have all of our younger selves there inside us. If we live long enough, we will experience many, many selves.

Somewhere inside every mature woman is a little child who wants to create, to play, to be free, to let go of the world of doing, and to just have fun. Author Eda LeShan wrote, "A nice little nap in the afternoon, with an arm around a teddy bear, followed by cookies and milk, feels just as good at eighty as it did at three." She also said, "Inside me there is surely a child I have worked hard to keep alive, to help me understand myself."

Let's face it, it's a great release to let yourself go, to sing and dance, to play games, or to do whatever else takes your fancy, without worrying about what someone might think. Reactivating the creative, playful child that is still within you is essential to successful aging.

If you watch a child play, you will notice that children delight at such innocent simple things, and so can you. Tell yourself that you're never too old to do anything your body will allow. After many years of being pulled in many different directions by spouse, children, biological and hormonal changes, and life, give your inner child permission to reemerge after her long sleep.

Write a letter to your inner child, and give her permission to be part of your life.

14
our work

*Your work is to discover your work and then with all your heart
to give yourself to it.*

—BUDDHA

The concept of the golden years originated as a public-relations program designed to make sixty-somethings feel good about their forced ousting from the workplace. In fact, retirement isn't a natural part of the human life cycle. It annoys me that retirement was, and still is, a social engineering experiment designed to move older, supposedly useless workers out of the workplace to make room for the young.

On the positive side, though, as a retiree or person nearing retirement, you now have the opportunity to go where your heart leads you. You can also get lost or run in circles. To know where you're going and how to get there, you need a map. Even if you look forward to retirement, you're giving up an identity and need to create a new one.

When you engage in what you were put on this earth to do, the activity is exhilarating and interesting. The work begets energy, health, and happiness while also helping to deflect tension and stress.

As a woman ages, a sense of urgency may grow as it becomes more important to do something meaningful and satisfying with the remainder of her life. Where do you go next? Attend art school? Take a computer class? Start a home business? In the grip of life's demands—making a living, serving a family's needs—it's easy to lose a sense of self. But it's always there—a thread of identity that runs from childhood through all the years following. Making good choices means discovering your true passions and what gives you true joy.

I like what Lavinia Russ wrote: "When death comes for me, I hope I'll be so busy working and laughing, I won't hear his knock. He'll have to break down the door to get in."

REACTIVATE YOUR DREAM

This is the real fear . . . not death or decrepitude but the dread that you'll inevitably turn into someone else, someone who doesn't live an exciting life or have exciting dreams.

—Barbara Sher

If your earliest career decisions were driven by the need to make money or a life decision to be at home with your family, the second half of your life can be driven by the fondest desires that you set aside in your youth. If the social and financial pressures of making money had never existed, what would you have done differently?

At some point, many women feel unfulfilled in their lives or their careers, no matter how successful they feel they've been. To revisit and reactivate your dreams without giving up what you have achieved so far, begin by imagining that you no longer need to win approval for being beautiful, strong, or successful.

Notice what you love—reading magazines, listening to music, playing tennis, being in the country. These loves are clues to your hidden desires. Many of your dreams may have come true already, and some may not be important anymore. The point is, you need to reconnect with your inner passions and find practical ways to act on them.

Break the pursuit down into small, manageable steps, and explore them one at a time. This gentle process will help you move closer to feeling satisfied with your life. It will also allow you to recognize early on that a dream may no longer be worth the effort it would take to make it so. A step-by-step approach will let you see that there are many different ways to enjoy your dream. For example, you can pursue your passion to be a writer by taking classes in the evening . . . or by merely reading about what steps other authors have taken to become published. Taking a class would give you with the fulfillment that comes from taking one step toward realizing your dream.

What dream would you like to reactivate? What small step can you take today toward living your passion?

DOING WHAT YOU LOVE

Trust in what you love, continue to do it, and it will take you where you need to go.

—Natalie Goldberg

I read in the *Los Angeles Times* that an eighty-year-old woman started parachute jumping when she was seventy-five. This fearless woman is representative of thousands of venturesome women in America who have passed well beyond the half-century mark. Some are blessed with good health and are determined to continue what they've always done, or what they've always wanted to do.

I don't enjoy the concept of mortality—or jumping out of planes, for that matter. However, thinking about the limited time we do have on this planet focuses my attention on how to meaningfully and effectively spend the days that are left. So here's the pivotal question: how do we discover our own natural talents and apply them in today's world?

Amy, a fifty-six-year-old mother and veterinarian, told me she thought about what she wanted to do all the time—sketch and paint—

but was waiting until the kids were fully out on their own to do it. Other women told me they didn't have enough time to figure out what they would do if they had the time.

Try not to be fearful; listen to your inner whisperings; allow your higher power to guide you. Author Sarah Ban Breathnach wrote, "Essentially what happens when you begin to do what you love is that you get a new employer: Spirit."

You've had rich life experiences, and you've acquired an extensive array of interests and abilities. Based on your life experiences, ask yourself: *What do I like? What do I do well?* By selecting job, volunteer, or career opportunities that fit your personal values, skills, and ideal work environment, you will achieve lasting satisfaction and a sense of self-worth. What things interest you most? What skills give you the most satisfaction and energy? Take stock of your present options, and create a vision for your future.

Consider creating a bridge between your spiritual self and your life's work. This means taking the essence of who you are and what you believe into your work space. If kindness, patience, honesty, and generosity are spiritual qualities that you believe in, make every effort to practice them in what you do.

What did you want to be when you were a younger girl, before someone insensitive told you it wasn't possible?

DO YOU HAVE A CALLING?

*I believe there's a calling for all of us. . . . The real work of our
lives is to become aware. And awakened. To answer the call.*

—OPRAH WINFREY

Do you have a calling? A calling is about your vocation, whether it is work, relationship, lifestyle, or service. It's about the search for personal meaning, which is a major developmental task of aging. Your heart may be calling you to do something (become self-employed, go back to school, volunteer, leave or start a relationship, move to the country, or change careers, for example). Your soul may be calling you to be something (more creative, less judgmental, more loving, or less fearful).

You may feel that insurmountable obstacles are getting in your way. Many women hesitate to answer an authentic calling because they're caught between the circumstances of their lives and creative choice. If you have it in your heart to play the piano, start a business, paint a picture, write a poem, or sing a song, then find a way to do it; don't let anything stop you.

Remember that you were born with the potential for the unfolding of your true self. If you deviate from that truth, you interfere with the intention of something far greater than you are, and as a result, you run the risk of developing discomfort in your body and psyche. In fact, the symptoms of anxiety might be regarded as a message from a powerful force within you that wants you to be yourself.

Most women yearn to know their purpose in life. Perhaps your calling has to do with service to others. We come into life with nothing, and we leave it with nothing. The truth is, we can't take what we acquire and achieve with us. The most important thing you can do with your life is give to others. Whenever you feel lost or unsure, remind yourself that your purpose is about giving. Direct your thoughts away from yourself, and spend the next few hours looking for ways to be of service to someone or something else.

Here is some wisdom from one of my favorite authors, Helen Nearing, who at eighty-nine wrote, "The universe is immense and gorgeous and magnificent. I salute it. Every speck, every little fly on the window salutes the Universe. Every leaf has its meaning. I think the Universe is expanding—it is experiencing and accomplishing. And we have the opportunity to add to its glow."

If money and time were no obstacle, what would you be doing with your life?

THE ENTREPRENEURIAL SPIRIT

Age teaches us it's our duty to be and do what we love.

—MARSHA SINETAR

Think you're too old to risk becoming an entrepreneur? At your age, you have a lifetime of practical experience. If you have good energy and a financial cushion to tide you over until your business catches on, you could do just fine. Do you have what it takes to succeed as an entrepreneur? There are five principles that make for successful entrepreneurship: experience at an early age (working for other entrepreneurs, starting a small business as a child, and so on), finding niche opportunities, building a strong team of associates, making friends with bankers and suppliers, and understanding financial statements. And one other attribute that women especially have an abundance of—intuition. Women entrepreneurs also tend to be more interested in self-fulfillment than in money and power, which adds to their success rate.

As with so many things in life, your attitude will determine whether or not you'll be a success as an entrepreneur. You have to be able to stay motivated through ups and downs in whichever business venture you embark upon. You have to trust in your decisions and think positively. Your attitude will also rub off on those around you.

You may not be able to do all the work yourself, so you must be willing to put a certain amount of confidence in those you'll be working with. Keep in mind that some things won't get done unless you do them yourself. When you're on your own, the buck stops with you.

Be realistic. You can't expect to receive a regular paycheck for a while. Can you stay sane when you don't have a guaranteed flow of income? Money may be very tight in your start-up years. If you're looking merely to supplement your retirement income, you might want to consider taking a part-time job rather than setting up your own business. If you decide to start a business, be sure you've put away enough money to live on during the slow times.

Find the right business for you, one that fits your lifestyle and personality, one that is a good match with your talents and experience. Being your own boss can put a strain on your health, so make sure you find ways to alleviate stress.

Don't overlook the value of writing a detailed business plan. You need the plan as your guide, and you will also need the plan if you want to raise start-up funds. Check your local library for helpful resources.

The worst that can happen is that your business fails, as 50 percent do in the first year, according to AARP. So what? At the least, you will have learned a lot that can be applied to a new business opportunity.

Have you ever had an idea for a business? What steps could you take to make your idea a reality?

WORKING RETIREMENT

I think the term "retirement" . . . is much too negative. . . .
"Recreatement" sounds much more encouraging.

—Helen Hayes

As people stay healthier and more active, many choose to work past the retirement age fixed by society's expectations or social security. Some of us simply enjoy working because it creates a sense of fulfillment. A lot of us are still working and plan to keep on working as long as we can to survive economically. One good reason to stay in the workforce is that retirement savings, pensions, and Social Security payments may not be enough to provide the comfortable lifestyle we want.

We can work for money if we want or need to, or we can give back to society in some way. The most youthful and interesting people I know in retirement are those who are not concentrating primarily on themselves. If and when you do retire from a paid job, a new world of volunteer activities opens up. Nonprofits frequently need and welcome older volunteers because they appreciate their skills and know that they're reliable.

Longevity will most likely bring you choices about work. It's important to think about those choices and what you'd most like to do in your later life.

What kind of "recreatement" do you envision for your retirement years?

TOO YOUNG TO RETIRE

The idea that one should retire never crosses my mind. I hope I'll always be writing and physically active.

—Elinor Gadon

As baby boomers reach retirement age, the growth of the workforce will slow sharply or stop, while demand for workers will continue to grow. Available jobs may outnumber workers by more than 4 million—rising to 35 million by 2031, according to AARP statistics. There will be more opportunities in the future for older women to have second careers if they want them.

I'm looking to older friends and authors for inspiration. In her inspiring book *On My Own at 107,* Sarah L. Delany wrote, "I don't see why folks should retire at sixty-five. I retired at seventy myself and looking back on it, I bet I could have kept teaching for a long, long while yet."

Do I want to retire like my eighty-year-old friends Len and Tita, high up in the mountains in their Swiss chalet–type log home near one of their married sons, surrounded by grandchildren? Len's working as a part-time minister in two local churches, and Tita's reading to herself, reading to the grandchildren, doing crafts, and running a Bible study once a week. Lots of homemade cookies for visitors, lots of busy-ness on Sundays.

Or do I want to retire like Maxine and Jim, spending six months each year in very affordable New Zealand and six months in very expensive, tax-burdened Westchester County, New York? In New Zealand, Jim has built and manages a theater and continues his meditation practice; Maxine continues to work in the investment and financial planning field and has opened a muffin shop. They both love to travel and will make time for it.

Or do I want to retire, like John and Sheila do in the beautiful house on the coast of Maine that they rent out part of the year? When they're not in Maine, they live in their mortgage-free house in New Rochelle, New York. Sheila's a full-time professor and writer; John's a part-time, retired clergyman invested in social action projects. Back and forth they travel from house to house with a walk or two around Europe thrown in.

So what is retirement anyway? Mary Baker Eddy was still the head of the Christian Science Church at age eighty-nine, and Coco Chanel was still CEO of her fashion company at the age of eighty-five.

What are your thoughts on retiring?

TOO OLD TO GET A JOB?

The idea that we are used up at sixty-five . . . is patently ridiculous. Why waste the experience of a lifetime?

—Joan Borysenko

You think you're too old to walk into a business and apply for a job? You're not. Millions of women over age fifty are taking up new careers, especially in areas that welcome mature workers. Work has no upper age limit. In fact, about 255,000 women in their seventies or older are still on the job.

Some work because they have to, but many work just to keep themselves feeling involved in life. Older women who find a job that gives them cash and contentment are the women who know what they like and what they enjoy. They've found more than cash and contentment. They've found freedom.

By law, if you want to work, you can't be denied a job, a promotion, or any job-related benefits solely because of your age. Contact the Equal Employment Opportunity Commission if you have questions or concerns.

If you really want to work, you can register with a temp firm that cares more about your experience and skills than your age. Sometimes a temp job can even lead to a permanent position if you want one.

Here's another idea. If you're retired and haven't worked in some time and are interested in doing some kind of job or starting a new career, take a look at the latest *Occupational Outlook Handbook* at your local library. This handbook, updated every two years, contains descriptions of about 250 jobs—earning potential, training and educational needs, skills required, working conditions, and other facts.

When you fill out a job application, don't give your date of birth. Employers can't ask your age, and you don't have to tell. Stress your accomplishments first and any volunteering you've done. Remember that skills can come from outside the workplace. If you stopped working to raise a family, list relative activities such as your ability to multitask, budget, and organize. And remember, 50 to 70 percent of people still get their jobs by networking.

If you were to apply for a job, what life skills would you bring to the table?

WHAT NOW?

Set your sights high, the higher the better. Expect the most wonderful things to happen, not in the future but right now.

—Eileen Caddy

Every age offers something you haven't experienced before (and I'm not talking about wrinkles and arthritis). At every age, you have an opportunity to star in your own adventure, to write and produce your own play. You can decide if life is an adventure or a chore.

Sometimes our life's purpose and success sneak up on us unexpectedly, as with Liz Smith, columnist and TV journalist, who said, "The best thing that happened to me in old age was that I got to be successful after I was about to retire."

You have choices. Or do you want to follow conventional wisdom and fall back on a model of dependency? Do you find yourself spending a lot of energy lamenting your youth—energy that you could be putting into your next venture?

What are your thoughts on staying involved and engaged in the world?

15
our finances

As a group, we're markedly different from previous older genera-
tions who pinched pennies and saved them all.

—JOAN RATTNER HEILMAN

To be honest, I wanted to leave this section out of the book. I just didn't
want to deal with the topic. Financial issues aren't easy to face no matter
what age you are. But whatever your circumstances might be, it's never
too late to take stock of how you're managing your financial resources.
We need to plan for change and find the information that will assist us
in carrying out our plans.

Money doesn't buy happiness, yet one reason we spend so much
of it on status-defining goods in the first place is probably because we
haven't figured out other ways to make ourselves happy. Unfortunately,
we may be overly influenced by the good life presented in advertise-
ments. Also, when it comes to happiness, what we spend our money
on can matter more than how much of it we have. Studies have shown
that putting more cash toward experiences rather than stuff, buying
a gift for someone else rather than for ourselves, and anticipating big
purchases longer makes us happier.

Most of us will experience the challenge of financial woes at some
point in our lives. But what else is new? As women, haven't we been

the ones with the clever ideas around budgeting and stretching a dollar until it snaps like a rubber band?

Life is chock-full of uncertainties. You don't know how long you'll live. You don't know what investment returns you'll earn. You don't know what inflation will be down the road. You don't know if next year will be a bear market or a bull market. Few of us want to deal with these unknowns. But anyone who's been down and out at some time in their lives (including this author) will tell you that the lean time was also a time of great resourcefulness.

This chapter will take only a broad look at the general legal and financial topics we must consider as we age. What I've written is by no means inclusive; it's just a place to start.

GETTING ADVICE

Growing older means learning to become good at giving up in some areas to gain new strengths in others.

—KATIE FUNK WIEBE

I have a gnawing feeling in my gut that just won't quit. About three months ago, I made an appointment with a financial planner—a woman I trust. My husband and I promised to assemble and give her our vital financial information so she could work up an analysis and give us some recommendations. Every time I think I'll sit down and get it all together, the anxiety builds and I run to the refrigerator to visit my food friends. Cheesecake never asks you about your financial future.

To top it off, I just finished reading an article by Terence Reed, author of *The 8 Biggest Mistakes People Make with Their Finances Before and After Retirement,* in which he says:

Mistake: Not putting your plans in writing.
Mistake: Being unrealistic about your exposure to risk.
Mistake: Neglecting to do "dignity planning."
Mistake: Closing the door on long-term-care insurance.

Mistake: Failing to understand the goal of estate planning.

Mistake: Stepping into tax traps that trip up retirement planning.

Mistake: Assuming you're too old for life insurance.

Too many mistakes to live with, and the article didn't even include the eighth one. Now I'm going to spend my sleepless nights wondering about that!

I need help. We all do on these matters. I'm promising myself I will call the financial planner next week. Maybe I can get her to come and hold my hand a bit more. I can't be the only woman she's ever met with financial anxiety.

If you haven't already, what will you do to get the financial advice you need?

GIVING TO YOUR KIDS WHILE YOU'RE STILL ALIVE

It's not your duty to pay for your child's education. It is your duty to give your child an education about money.

—Suze Orman

I love my grown kids, and I'd give them the world if I could, but it seems as if every time I turn around, they need a loan for something important. I don't remember asking my parents for more than a couple hundred dollars to put down on my first car, a 1967 Volkswagen Beetle (new, it cost $1,979). After their help with the small down payment, I don't remember ever going back to them for more. Has the world changed so much? Doesn't it seem that our adult children are more financially dependent than we were?

When you loan money to your adult children, assume you will never be paid back. Even well-meaning children will put you at the bottom of their list of creditors. If you have the means, you might consider family loans as gifts. This prevents hurt feelings and strained relationships when the loan is not repaid.

As for leaving money to your children when you die, here is one caution. If, for one reason or another, you disinherit a child, you guarantee that the child's only memories of you will be bad ones. Consider that if one child is left more than another, despite the fact there may be good reasons for this move, you may ruin their future relationships with one another.

When it comes to money and your adult children, I say help them out a bit when you can while you're alive and only when it's appropriate. If you can afford to, why not give them some happiness and security while you're around to see it?

What are your thoughts and feelings on this topic?

HELPING YOUR AGING PARENTS

The great lesson to be learned in this last developmental stage is acceptance. That lesson well learned brings serenity. In the end, everything is about love.

—MARY PIPHER

About 7 million Americans care for their aging parents. I'm not one of them. Both of my parents have passed on, so I don't have some of the difficult issues around their finances that some of you face.

You might have to pay bills or balance the checkbook for your parents. To help maintain their dignity, allow them to sign the checks or review what you've done. If you live far away and can't monitor the bills easily, ask the utility and telephone companies to put emergency third-party notifications on the accounts. If any bills ever go into default, you would be notified before service is shut off. Many companies will do this for elderly account holders.

If you suspect your parents are being financially exploited, don't adopt a wait-and-see approach. Try to be vigilant about signs of exploitation like large withdrawals, unauthorized ATM use, or a new name added to the account. Ask your parents to let you run a credit check on them every so often to see if any new accounts or lines of credit have been opened in their name without their knowledge. Ask your parents if they will allow a financial advisor to conduct annual checkups of their portfolio and insurance policies to prevent trouble.

You may be reluctant to bring up the issue of estate planning with your parents because you don't want to appear greedy. Remind them that if they haven't made provisions, the state will apply its own formula for distribution of the estate and the state won't respect their wishes.

If your parents are still living, in what ways would it be appropriate for you to help them with their finances?

LIVING WELL ON LESS

Why give the money to the stores? Keep it for yourself.

—GRANDMA AGDA

Are you one of those people who hates to be called a senior? Get over it. You may be getting older, but once you hit the designated birthday, you become eligible for an astonishing number of great deals simply for having lasted so long. Whether you are offered these discounts out of respect for your age or because someone realized it was a major marketing tool, you'd be crazy not to take advantage of what's available.

I know a few women who refuse to ask for a senior citizen's ticket at the movies or any senior discount whatsoever, and I think that's foolish. We're all getting older, and as author Frances Weaver says, "You're just ahead of the pack, right now." Carry proof of age with you. Join AARP, and they'll send you an ID card. Get a senior ID through your local Office for the Aging. This card entitles you to a wide array of discounts. Don't be afraid to ask for discounts wherever you shop.

Don't wait for anybody to volunteer information about your special privileges. Be bold. Ask if there's a senior discount. Some hotel chains offer half off the regular price—just about every lodging chain and most individual establishments in the country will give you a break if you're over fifty.

Other than senior discounts, there are myriad ways you can live well on less. Here are some ideas of my own and some I've gathered from a variety of sources:

- Don't go shopping unless you really need something. Buy only what you can afford.

- Take care of what you have, and don't throw out anything if it is still usable.

- Stop trying to impress people.

- Get by with one car, and keep it as long as possible. Shop around for auto insurance, and drop unnecessary coverage.

- Rent out space in your home or garage.

- Learn to shop at Goodwill, Salvation Army, garage sales, and thrift stores in your area.

- Try not to spend coins smaller than a quarter for routine purchases. Put the coins in a jar. With this "found money" you can get a massage, invest it, or take a class.

- Find a low-interest credit card and use it wisely. Credit card debt isn't a good idea at *any* age.

- Join a co-op to buy food in bulk. Buy meat when it's on sale and freeze it.

- Choose basic clothing styles that can be dressed up or down, and build your wardrobe around a few colors that look good on you.

- Use coupons for only what you would buy anyway.

- Call the local utility company for an energy audit, and take advantage of its cost-saving advice.

- Consider low-cost entertainment options such as early-bird dinners, college theater presentations, and inexpensive adult education classes.

- Make gifts more meaningful by passing on an item you already own.

- Check out books, audiotapes, DVDs, and music CDs from the library rather than buying them.

Before I buy anything, I imagine it sitting on a garage sale table. You'd be surprised how many times I've put an item back on the shelf after considering what I would be selling it for in ten years.

Which suggestions do you find yourself resisting?

MONEY AND STUFF

Another bonus to growing older is . . . a decreased interest in spending all that time and money shopping.

—Mary McConnell

I can't say it enough times: understand what's going on with your money. Unless you've been diagnosed with mental health issues or some other disability, don't give the job of primary money manager to someone else in your family. If you're sixty and suddenly find yourself alone, you'll feel anxious and overwhelmed if it's been twenty-five years since you've had anything to do with your finances. If you're married and your husband manages the finances, find out now what he is doing and how he does it. Know each other's passwords and PINs. If you share a safe-deposit box, make sure you know where the key is.

When in doubt, seek the advice of a trusted professional who is willing to hear your concerns and field your questions, no matter how silly they might be. How do you find a trusted professional? Ask some friends for a referral and check credentials with a related financial organization.

When you meet with a financial advisor, ask: If my husband dies before I do, what financial and legal steps should I take? What happens to my assets when I die? Do I need a living will? Should my will be updated, and if so, how often? Will I have enough to live on? Is it too late to start a savings program?

You'll want to have your important financial documents in a place where someone can find them if you become ill or die—documents such as your will, bank account information, a durable power of attorney, a medical power of attorney, insurance policies, and investment documents.

If you feel a bit daunted and overwhelmed by the subject of finances, you're not alone. Older women, especially those who have engaged in limited paid work or whose marital status has changed, are likely to have had little financial experience or education. Don't despair. You really don't need an advanced degree to achieve financial literacy.

What questions and concerns do you have? Will you find a professional to guide you?

PLANNING RETIREMENT

Rehearse your retirement . . . and try it out about five years before you plan to stop working.

—CHRISTINA POVENMIRE, FINANCIAL PLANNER

Staring us right in the face is the fact that we have a longevity bonus of roughly thirty years or so past sixty. The challenge is, what are we going to do with those bonus years? How are we going to spend them, and with what resources?

If you are married, the retirement phase of your life involves both of you, and any planning has to be done jointly. It's helpful to begin planning retirement years before you retire so you'll feel less stressed and there won't be disputes about how to spend your money. Agree in advance how you will adjust to retirement, from spending your time together in activities like travel to splitting chores to getting part-time jobs. Review finances to project how much you will have to spend, and agree on what to spend it on.

The goal-setting stage of planning is a time to dream and visualize your future. Do you want to travel? Move to a different place? Spend more time with your grandchildren? Launch your own business or a new career? Take up a new sport or hobby?

Calculate how much money you will have to live on during retirement, and try living on that amount for a time. You may find full-time retirement impractical, and part-time work may be necessary. A postretirement letdown can come from financial as well as emotional causes—a realization that your finances aren't providing the retirement you had anticipated. Be honest in your retirement planning so you know exactly how far your nest egg will carry you.

Anticipate the phases of retirement, and plan ahead for each. For most people, retirement will consist of four phases, with different comfort zones required for each.

The honeymoon phase of retirement typically ends six months to two years after you've taken the initial steps. And if you haven't prepared for what happens next, you may become depressed, feeling unimportant or unappreciated because you don't see yourself doing anything meaningful or significant. Start by making clear, long-range plans to go back to school, develop a second career, or involve yourself in community service. Build a structure that will sustain you when the honeymoon ends and the post-honeymoon letdown begins.

Then comes the active-living phase, when you're healthy, vigorous, and over the post-honeymoon letdown. Now you might be able to do the traveling you always hoped to do or go back to school.

Next is the slowing-down phase, when you're still pretty healthy, only now it's harder to get around. You might use this time for catching up on such long-deferred activities as organizing your family photographs, writing your memoirs, or telling your grandchildren how you lived as a child. You might still want to travel, but tours will be more your speed.

The fourth phase is the assisted-living phase. Let's face it—none of us wants to think we will someday be dependent on others for help. But we will need some assistance when we become old and infirm, so plan for it, but don't spend your retirement years obsessing about it.

In your journal, start by writing answers to the following: What do you want to have, to do, to be, and to see during your retirement years? How will you continue to feel worthwhile and valuable to society? Will you continue working part time, or will you volunteer for a charity?

WEALTH AND HAPPINESS

There are so many other ways to feel rich in your later years that have nothing at all to do with financial wealth.

—Debbie, age 74

I'm happy when I wake up to blue skies in the spring. There's no admittance charge for that view of the sky. I'm happy when I smell homemade bread baking. I'm happy when I see the smiles on my grandchildren's faces (priceless). Of course, I'm also happy when I can pay my bills.

Then there are times when I sit down to pay my bills and thoughts run in my head like, *What will I be able to afford when I'm seventy-five? Will I have to give up my occasional trip to Chico's for a new t-shirt? Will I be eating Cheerios and peanut butter sandwiches for three meals a day?*

I learned something about this in my research. It seems those who were happiest in their later years were not necessarily wealthy. As our culture has become more affluent, we haven't gotten any happier. Even though Americans earn twice as much in today's dollars as they did in 1957, the proportion of those who say they are very happy has declined. What does that tell you? We spend a majority of our first fifty years trying to achieve and accumulate wealth and material goods, but it doesn't buy us any long-lived happiness.

As we age, we can find another way to calculate our worth other than that of money earned. These days, I'm so much more aware of what really matters. The designer handbag that I thought was so important to have when I was thirty sits on a shelf in my closet collecting dust as a reminder of how many hours I had to work to buy it. What was I thinking? Most likely, I was hoping that someone would notice my wonderful bag and think that I was officially successful.

I imagine that, like so many American women, I won't be able to afford every material thing I'd like in the future, but what in the world is it (besides health care and food) that I need anyway?

How do you feel about this?

part IV

16
looking forward

Paradoxical as it may seem, to believe in youth is to look backward; to look forward we must believe in age.

—Dorothy L. Sayers

Author Gail Sheehy once said, "I'm aware of looking for my future self and I think that's something women in their fifties begin to do." My sister describes her experience of meeting with and accepting her future self in this poem:

The Message

I wanted to take the old woman's hand in mine
touch future-perfect version of my unmet self
to comfort her . . . and me
restore life-force through her bony hand
to reach her heart . . . and mine
as if through sheer belief my love
could touch, restore faith, release the lock
of time upon her heart . . . and mine
She passed and turned to look at me
driftwood in her eyes

a knowing smile released her face
as if she could read my intention
as if we had broken the code to acceptance
as if she understood my wish
for her . . . and me
From a stranger on a crowded autumn train . . .
an unexpected gift
waiting to be opened.

—Marilyn Houston

The next years will be an interesting time for our society. When a growing percentage of the population lives past one hundred, we will see what happens to the psychological and spiritual direction of our culture. As we move into the future, we will be redefining aging. After we battle the cultural attitudes that try to define us and attempt to stall us out, we will be staying involved in life in any way we can—volunteering, working, growing, creating, discovering, and enjoying our lives.

What will our world be like in the next decades? If we don't get run over by a bus, we have a good chance of achieving very old age. Diseases, accidents, and illness will be treated in very advanced ways. In the years to come, replacing diseased or worn-out body parts will be as routine as replacing auto parts today. A scan of your genetic structure will detect symptoms or susceptibility to particular diseases. Nanobots, minuscule robots, will deliver medications to affected cells to prevent or treat disease—they'll clear clogged arteries or repair damaged tissue. You'll have all your vital signs tested by drugstore machines, which send the results to your doctor via the Internet for analysis. Implanted biochips will monitor your vital signs, alerting you or your doctor to an impending crisis.

As we work to balance our physical, emotional, and spiritual lives, navigating the years ahead will require us to keep an open mind about technological advances. For example, imagine you are seated in a special chair that senses if you're cold or uncomfortable and adapts accordingly. Then you pull a bubble screen down around you, and as you sit relaxed and comfortable, your computer/entertainment center will be programmed to teach you any language you want, produce a jazz bass line to go with your computerized melody, or let you play a round of virtual reality golf.

Even as we look forward, we must not leave the richness of our past to atrophy on a dusty shelf. We can learn so much from revisiting where we have been. We're not meant to regret and dwell on the past, but we shouldn't live only in the moment. It's easier to move forward if you take the time to stop, look back, and take an inventory of all those times you didn't listen to yourself so you can learn from them.

In this book, we have faced transitions in our relationships with ourselves, our families, and our communities. We've realized that there is no set chronological point at which old age begins and that creativity is not just the domain of the young. In these pages, we've explored our health and our wholeness on more than one level, addressing our feelings as well as our intellect, our bodies as well as our minds.

The first step toward successful aging begins with a realistic assessment of our current life situation and the challenges that will undoubtedly confront us in the future. The choice not to choose is the choice to live irresponsibly. If we do not choose our activities and attitudes with clear judgment coming from a courageous and realistic assessment of our lives and circumstances, we fall into choosing unconsciously and poorly, and we will pay a hard price.

In the pages that follow, you will be asked to consider the future in a variety of ways, including any dreams you still have for yourself, what it takes to start over after loss or disappointment, and what you need to let go of in order to move forward. You will be asked to consider and respond to what it means to accept your humanity, what changes you can make to enhance your life, what you've learned from your past, and what you can do to inspire the younger generation by leaving a lasting legacy.

FUTURE DREAMS

The future belongs to those who believe in the beauty of their dreams.

—Eleanor Roosevelt

Just because I'm older doesn't mean I have to stop dreaming about the future. I want my old age to be different from my youth, not just a continuation of it. In looking back over my life, I understand that actions I once thought praiseworthy actually caused harm, and things I judged harshly simply indicated an innocent narrow-mindedness at the time. As I grow older and perhaps wiser, the meaning of life rests more on my willingness to see that some goals were not as important as I thought them to be.

As you live longer, you will start to see the earlier dramas, treasures, and goals of your life as part of a learning curve—a learning experience that's been neither wonderful nor awful.

Writing something down makes it real. Your words about your future goals and dreams become magical messengers as your hands inscribe the thoughts in your brain as well as on paper. When you use this method to seek your goals, something special happens—it works. Through writing, the subconscious lets us know what we want. Author Marsha Norman wrote, "Dreams are . . . illustrations from the book your soul is writing about you."

Think about your dreams of the future. What is your soul writing about you?

THE FREEDOM TO CHANGE

As some people age, they grow nostalgic for yesteryear. Not me . . .
I am just hitting my stride.

—DELLA REESE

To everything there is a season. Whether we like our lives as they are or wish for change, the first universal law is that nothing stays the same. This nonnegotiable fact propels us through a lifetime of difficult leave-takings and exhilarating renewals. The most significant changes are wrought by the awesome force of time. Without any concerted effort on our part, time will make us wiser and gentler.

Sooner or later, we find that we lose our breath walking up a hill that once posed no challenge. We glance at the reflection of an aging woman in a store window and discover with shock that we are that woman. Although time will impose its natural changes on your body and soul, you still have control and freedoms at this age that you never had before.

We all have two lives: the one we learn with and the one we live with after that. If the one life you have been living with is begging for change, now is not the time to be cautious in exploring new parts of yourself.

In your journal, write in as much detail as you can how you would like to change and evolve during the next years of your life.

FEELING NEW AGAIN

When a woman conceives her true self, a miracle occurs and life around her begins again.

—MARIANNE WILLIAMSON

In *On My Own at 107,* Sarah L. Delany reports, "Just when it seemed winter might never end, I ventured outdoors and was greeted by a wondrous sight: Bessie's crocus plants were peeking through the snow." Sarah's sister Bessie had planted the crocuses years before her death, when she was already more than one hundred years old. Their flowering reminded Sarah of a philosophy they'd once shared. Bessie and Sarah, sisters who were devoted to each other and their professional careers, felt that each new day was a blessing, a chance to be new again.

If you're going to embrace the concept of feeling new each day, perhaps the symbolism of a crocus "peeking through the snow" will inspire you as it did me. Crocuses start out as wrinkled little turd-like orbs. They sleep frozen in the earth for months of cold weather, yet have the audacity to live through it and timidly peek through the ground to display their fragile flowers once again!

So you may be feeling a bit like a turd. Go for a walk, and notice something beautiful along the way. Get your hair done, and ask the hairdresser to massage your neck. Get yourself a touring bike, and go for a ride. Pick apples at an orchard. Notice the trees budding in spring, help out at a children's home. Try a yoga class for mature women. Look for ways to feel new again.

What can you do to change your outlook on life and feel new again?

DOORS AND WINDOWS

*Doorways are sacred to women for we are the doorways of life
and we must choose what comes in and what goes out.*

—MARGE PIERCY

I've heard that the eyes are the windows of the soul and when one door closes, another opens. Joan Rivers once said, "If I can't make it through one door, I'll go through another door—or I'll make a door. Something terrific will come no matter how dark the present." Joseph Campbell said that when you "follow your bliss," doors you never knew were there will open to you.

Every life event is a door to discovering more about ourselves. No matter what our age, we need to look for these doors because they are waiting for us to find them. Today is the beginning of the rest of your life, and it's a good time to ask how many doors are still left for you to open—and which windows need cleaning. Windows and doors have opened and shut, gotten stuck, and at times, the key to unlocking them has been lost altogether.

You are more than your crow's-feet, and you are more than the wrinkles on your eyelids. Doors will continue to swing open when you keep a positive outlook, when you follow your passions.

Begin to make plans for the rest of your life—one window, one door at a time. Make an effort to discover which doors are still open to you, which ones will need to be locked shut, what kind of windows you want to look through, and which offer you a better view toward the rest of your life.

In your journal, write about which metaphorical doors you'd like to close, which ones you'd like to open, and which windows need cleaning.

BECOMING HUMAN

I feel like, God expects me to be human. I feel like, God likes me just the way I am: broken and empty and bruised.

—C. JoyBell C.

I'm human, all right! I know because some days are easier than others. I know because I don't sleep as well as I used to, or because the senior moments get the better of me and I can't find the humor (human) in it. Some days every bone crunches and scrapes against the others, and going upstairs seems a feat (or a defeat).

Of course, there are days when I'm bright and nimble. When the brain is crisp and functional, when the creaking bones aren't quite as noisy. When I love that my eyes are working well enough (with glasses, of course!) to read the good books and to see the bad movies. That my eyes may have trouble with the newspaper but can still read a good poem. That my eyes can hardly distinguish *1 cup* from *1 Tbsp.* in the cookbook but see well enough to eat. I love that my bones can be warmed by sipping English breakfast tea, that my teeth can still munch through a whole bag of trail mix. I love that I am able to write what I'm seeing and feeling and that I can hear music and laughter.

Today, I will not dwell on the times I have so little patience with myself that I want to evaporate into the heat of the sun. I love me, I love me not, I love me, I love me not. I'll turn up my light a little brighter. I'm human, and that's all right with me.

Are you having trouble accepting your humanness? Why?

HARVESTING THE PAST

I am like one sent away to gather the harvest, and now returning, baskets full. Enough, I think, to sustain me in the autumn and winter that is still ahead. Until I am gathered, at the end, into the Creator's own great harvest.

—Hilary Lohrman

The word *harvest* brings to mind images of a horn of plenty—of fruits and vegetables spilling out, overflowing with bright autumn colors, holding the promise of abundance and nourishment. I believe harvesting our past holds the same promise.

I remember conversations with a seventy-two-year-old friend of mine who was writing her memoirs. She remarked that as her short-term memory seemed to be misfiring, her long-term memory was firing up. Much to her amazement, she was recalling events she had not thought of since they'd occurred. She wrote about her firsts—her first love, pet, home, experience of death, disability, triumph—and found her life rich with resources she could use going forward.

When you harvest your past, you will undoubtedly come across an expanded frame of reference that offers your life a cohesive spiritual meaning. Joan Borysenko wrote, "The need for an older woman to tell and retell the stories of her life is no idle preoccupation with the past." She says that this is a vital process that helps us come to terms with events and experiences.

My twenties and early thirties were a challenging and intense time. At that time, I was a divorced single mom living on a very limited income. I see now that I gained a resourcefulness that may be needed in the future when I'm living on a retirement income. Although tough, those lean days thirty years ago were filled with joy and appreciation for the small things. Dinner out was an event planned and looked forward to for weeks. There was the anticipation of finally bringing home the sweater waiting on layaway for three months, and I remember the Christmas my daughter and I cut catalog pictures of those items we couldn't afford to buy for each other and pasted them into giftboxes we wrapped and put under the tree.

Author Melody Beattie says, "Value what you've learned in your past. Each lesson has led to the next." Each person and circumstance has been invaluable in shaping you into the person you are today.

Harvest your past with an intention to enrich your life. If you choose to see only what you haven't accomplished, the material things you never had, the roads you think you should have taken and didn't, then you are not harvesting the past for the positive lessons. Instead, you are pulling in negativity and filling your silos with moldy grain. Today, reap the rewards of your story, choose to gather in your personal wealth and celebrate the harvest.

Write about the people, places, events, and experiences that helped shape who you are. Harvest a story from your past, and tell how it's enriching your life today.

GET ON WITH LIVING

Life loves the liver of it.

—MAYA ANGELOU

Let's get on with living and with becoming intimate with our lives and what makes us happy. We may be overlooking the best things in life because we're focusing too hard on what doesn't matter. We put off doing what would make us happy.

How long are you going to save your good china for some special event? Isn't today a special event? Why deny yourself the luxury of eating a meal on that dinner plate rimmed in 24-karat gold?

What about your dress-up clothes? When was the last time you wore your velvet slacks just to go to the movies? How about that blue silk blouse that's been hanging in the back of the closet? Wouldn't it be fun to wear that to the supermarket? Can you see yourself pulling out your library card from the hand-beaded clutch you use once every five years when you attend a wedding?

What are you waiting for? How about the seventy-five-dollar bottle of perfume sitting on the dresser top, waiting to be used for a special night out? Why not spray some on before your next trip to the hardware store? Take off your beat-up sneakers, and wear your best shoes to meet your friend at the diner for pancakes.

I've made a promise to myself that I'm not going to waste another day. I'm planning a trip to Sweden to see what few relatives are still alive. I'm reading those books I bought two summers ago to read someday. I'm going shopping in my closet for dress-up clothes, and I'm going to wear them. The special occasion I've been waiting for is happening now at the picnic table in my own backyard. Tonight, I'll use the lace tablecloth. Tonight, I'll eat a hot dog on the good dishes.

How can you get on with living instead of waiting for life to happen?

STARTING OVER

Tell me how you start over again and again, rise like a phoenix from the ashes, resurrect yourself, and go forward.

—BettyClare Moffatt

At fifty-plus, we begin an entirely different part of our lives, and for many of us, it's a part so different, we hardly recognize it as being connected to the younger ones.

I remember thinking that the car accident I had at forty-nine was the end of life as I had known it. Unable to get my injured brain to function as it always had, I had to let go into a new way of being. I was forced to start over. I decided this close call with death was an opportunity to start over in a dramatic way. I was being forced to let go of the younger, frantic, overworked, ten-balls-in-the-air self and start a new life pace. Mary McConnell, author of *Still Dancing*, said it best when she wrote, "The women who seem most vital in their later years often are women who have been divorced, widowed, or have suffered some similar crisis in late middle age that got them moving in new ways."

Oprah Winfrey once said, "As I see it, if you have ignored anything in your life you should have paid attention to in this life—this second, moving into the third act—is the time to do it."

How do you feel about this?

A SUPPORT FOR THE YOUNG

She leaned against the old woman's knee as a support, a prop, drowned, enfolded, in warmth, dimness, and soft harmonious sounds.

—V. SACKVILLE-WEST

I like the idea of being the place someone can come to lean against for a while, that my "old woman's knee" could be a support for a wounded soul—that who I am could provide a soft place to fall for a younger person.

Author Marianne Williamson wrote, "In our sixties and seventies, we could, in addition to shining, start teaching others, those coming up after us, how to do what we have done." Give it some thought. Is there an organization in your town that could use a volunteer to mentor someone younger? Is there someone in your family, or your friends' families, who would benefit by your spending a little extra time listening to them? What about your own children and grandchildren? Are you a support and a soft place for them to be vulnerable and not judged?

I know that when my day includes a moment or two of helping or inspiring someone younger, I feel purposeful and more alive—as if some of their youngness has rubbed off on me.

In what way can you be supportive to someone younger?

LIVING FOREVER

I know I don't want to live forever—but I wonder what it would feel like.

—ANNE, AGE 51

Suppose you had a choice: would you rather live out your expected life span—currently about eighty-five years for a woman—or live 122 years, the longest documented human life? A range of new findings is snapping into focus the prospect of a radically new science of aging—one that points toward the possibility of lengthening the human life span by relatively simple manipulation of a small number of genes. Excitement is mounting among biologists that the secrets of longer life will be discovered in the next two decades. Many biologists say it's conceivable that human beings could be rejiggered to live 150 to 160 years.

For all the excitement, science doesn't yet have answers to the most fundamental questions about aging. For example, what are the biological factors that determine why people age differently? Scientists imagine that aging will be slowed either by surgery, such as stem cell or gene therapy, or by taking a pill that will replace tissues and organs in our bodies with new ones made from our own cells.

Of course, controversy rages. Should society license drugs against aging? At what age should people take them? At eighteen, forty-five, sixty-five? What side effects to the body and brain should be considered acceptable?

Roy Walford, a pathologist and author of *Beyond the 120-Year Diet,* believes that humans might one day achieve immortality by changing how we eat. The diet he proposes, however, will make people skinnier, more tired, unable to sit on hard chairs, less interested in sex, and hungrier. Yeah, sure, that sounds like fun!

In the future, it may be mandatory for people to have some of their cells banked (maybe at birth), and when they get sick or start having aches and pains, they'll say to their doctor, "Doc, could you order up some new cartilage for me? My knees hurt." Then, after the cartilage is "cooked," it's injected into their knees and they instantly get a new lease on quality and length of life.

We could become the first generation to control our own destiny, a position that human beings have never before occupied. Some say that if we can prevent old age, why not? If we can prevent suffering, why not? Why not live to see your grandchildren and their children grow up?

If you could live a very long life, would you? Why?

LEAVING A LEGACY

If I do have a fantasy, it's in the role of young people coming to me and my being able to share with them some of the wisdom I've gained.

—Jane Goodall

We older women have a particular hard-won wisdom that we've gleaned through consciously processing the experiences of our lives. What are we going to do with this wisdom? Play canasta on Tuesdays, bingo on Wednesdays? We have an opportunity, and a responsibility on some level, to be mentors for the younger generation.

Mentoring doesn't always go smoothly. Sometimes it's like dancing when the partners step on each other's toes. If you insist on dispensing wisdom regardless of someone's readiness or willingness to receive, the younger person won't be receptive. Go slowly; trust takes time.

Mentors shouldn't impose doctrines and values on the people they mentor in an attempt to clone themselves. Instead, they foster others' individuality, applauding them as they struggle to clarify their own values and discover their authentic life paths. We bless them in the heroic, worthwhile, and difficult task of becoming more than they would have become alone. We encourage them by saying, "So what if you made a mistake? You can start again."

In the pursuit of leaving a lasting legacy, cultivate the art of attentive listening, carefully portioning out comments and thoughtful questions. Real communication occurs when you've taken the time to tune in to the other.

In this exchange, communication is a two-way process from which both parties benefit. You will find the younger person's vitality will rejuvenate and invigorate you as you share in her energy and fresh ideas. Meanwhile, the younger person receives perspective and a readiness to bridge the past and future.

The legacy you leave can also be as simple as passing on your story or your treasures. Martha McPhee wrote an essay titled "Blue Bowl of History," in which she recalls her grandmother: "She was determined that I know her stories, as if by learning them I'd carry her legacy forward, assuring her a certain immortality."

The happiest older women are those who readily give of themselves to younger generations. We all have unique gifts to share and pass on. Before you can capitalize on your uniqueness, though, you must have a good idea of what it is that makes you different.

In what ways are you unique? Take an inventory of your gifts and skills, and write about them in your journal. Where will you look to find someone to mentor?

FOR FUTURE GENERATIONS

Never doubt that a small group of thoughtful, committed citizens can change the world. Indeed, it is the only thing that ever has.

—Margaret Mead

Women in the new century won't be disappointed with the upcoming array of showstopping smart technologies intended to improve our everyday lives, but we may not be able to figure out how to use them! While I yearn for the convenience and aid of high-tech marvels, I'm not willing to completely give up my real books for words scrolling down a screen or a live concert at Carnegie Hall for the virtual-reality version.

Technology may extend human life spans by years, even decades. You could be married to your spouse for eighty or ninety years! Experts in an article from *Scientific American* say that computers will be able to calculate and think as well as the human brain by 2020, but do you want to own a machine that's smarter than you are?

Those same scientists predict that there will be something called an intelligent room that will have walls that can see and hear you and then speak to you in response to your requests. No more hiding out in secret with your box of Oreos without an intelligent room scolding you! They tell us that most household equipment, from TVs to toasters, will respond to voice commands. Guess you'll have to watch what you say to your microwave! They also say that smart cupboards and refrigerators will automatically reorder food that runs out. Can you imagine never running out of ice cream sandwiches? Electronic wallpaper will let us change the color and pattern of our walls instantly (wasn't that accomplished in the 1960s with drugs?).

Besides technological advances, what do we want to leave to future generations of women? In this moment, we are helping to shape the future of aging for every generation of women that follows after us.

We will show them that age can be free and joyous, that it's possible to live with pain and loss, that it's important to say what we really think and feel. We will show them that we know who we are, that we know more than we ever thought we would, that we're not afraid of what people think of us as we move with wonder into an unknown future.

Generativity is an adult's concern for and commitment to the well-being of future generations. It's the impulse to become more productive and to do more worthwhile things with their lives. We have opportunities to be generative in many different ways—as parents and grandparents, teachers or their assistants, mentors, leaders, friends, neighbors, and volunteers. Giving birth to a child is perhaps the most fundamental form of generativity. But people can metaphorically give birth to many things—from starting a business, to writing a poem, to painting a work of art, to coming up with a new solution to an old problem. Generativity is also about caring for the next generation. The task is to accept that we won't live forever and to seek to leave behind a positive legacy for the future.

Travelers on this road develop the virtue of caring, which paves the way to a rewarding second half of life. This valuable quality focuses on concern for others beyond the immediate family. It demonstrates practical concern for the younger generations and the quality of both social and environmental conditions that we are passing on to them. Caring can also be expressed through the development of thoughtful products, careful systems, quality literature, insightful art, concern for the planet's well-being, and more.

The choice to practice healthy caring expands our essential nature. We learn to accept ourselves with honesty, patience, and warmth. We fall in love with the beautiful child we once were. We enlarge the boundaries of our heart. "Carve your name on hearts, not tombstones. A legacy is etched into the minds of others and the stories they share about you," wrote Shannon L. Alder.

The good news is that we are given many opportunities to choose the road called generativity. It doesn't necessarily look peaceful or calm because change and growth can be disruptive. This road beckons us to be newly open to places, people, ideas, growth, beauty, dreams, hopes, giving, and rewards. When we are living according to this path in a way that is congruent with our inner core, we have chosen the route that will make all the difference in our own lives as well as in those around us.

In this book, you have learned to care for yourself in healthy ways, to simplify your life by taking time to reflect and gain insight, to clear away clutter and confusion. You have learned to set limits, and you have courageously explored both your inner self and the conditions around you. You have looked at your body, mind, and spiritual self as it relates to the aging process. You have examined your fears and imagined your future. You have begun to envision a better world for yourself, your friends, and your families. You have begun to imagine your future in such a way that you have become sensitized to the sacredness of your life on this earth.

I once read an African proverb that said, "The world was not left to us by our parents. It was lent to us by our children." What survives you and me are the world's children. I imagine them awaiting our wisdom. They are innocent and dependent on our ability to share what we have learned. The future looks to each of us with hope.

In your journal, write a letter that begins with "Dear future generations of women: My wish for you is . . ."

I leave you with this beautiful poem, written by my sister and inspired by our Swedish grandmother, who lived to be 102.

39 Fountain Place

Your black and white marble floors and 4th floor walkup
    stairs, cool to the touch
concave smoothness now, like some rundown monument
to forgotten immigrants, their accents mingling, reaching out
from acneed ecru walls and crushed, cracked tiles, their
misspelled names engraved in modern walls at Ellis Island.
Generations of bicycles, baby buggies, scooters and carts
have crammed your crud-stung caves in stairwells, damp,
sensuous lovers' kisses given and stolen there.
Stories sung and told in many different tongues
still echoing here, are layered in time, significant
remnants of flapper days, zoot-suit craze and prohibition,
purple haze and prostitution; but in earlier days,
war blackouts, ration stamps, Mayor LaGuardia reading
    funny papers,
modern plagues and evolution recorded in stone, plaster and
    lead-based

paint. Iceman, tinker, refugee, bring out your waste to the
    chanting
junkman, patiently plodding, ringing-bell nodding broken
    down
sway-back horse and jingly cart up Huguenot Street, wound
around and down North Avenue past the Lutheran Church
and back again like absent-minded clockwork
or an impossible 500-piece jigsaw puzzle on Gramma's card
    table,
redcoats on horses jumping hedges, hunting foxes, horns
    trumpeting,
hooves galloping, maidens waving handkerchiefs at the sun.
Tar paper roofs and horses hooves, indelible mind prints.
Even then there were no fountains.
Gramma's place, 4th floor walkup, is still there.
I almost knocked on her door last October, but was afraid to
    see who might be living there now,
knowing full well that her lacy curtains fresh from stretching
    dry on wooden racks,
and her hand-made doilies would be gone,
her dresser drawers so fresh with their soapy scented silky-
    white
cotton sheets ironed and folded just so,
would not be there anymore.
The bedroom where once I tasted her perfume and spit it out
    the window,
where I wrote my name in powder on her mirrored dressing
    table top.
Oriental rug living room floor where we slept on those scent-
    ed white sheets
on steaming nights with no cross ventilation at all.
Small kitchen where the iceman put the block
and mom fed me pablum so fast that I choked.

Sometimes Gramma smoked a cigarette,
blowing the smoke out that kitchen window.
Where the toaster sat on oilcloth, its angled,
tipping sides always overcooking the bread
so we had to scrape the black off before eating it.
I'm sure a speck of her raspberry jam lies somewhere
on the woodwork beneath 50 coats of paint.
The closet in her room where the monster lived,
bright glowing eyes, may be living among
synthetics now, instead of wool and mothballs.
Deep white tub, wooden tugboats
in a sea of bubbles, her calling,
"don't stand up in the tub until I get there,"
Strauss playing on the radio . . .
Oh, God, how I miss her.

—MARILYN HOUSTON

acknowledgments

First and foremost, a big thank-you to my very talented poet-friend-sister-editor, Marilyn Houston, for her contributions to this book; to Debra Meryl Cerbini, a multitalented assistant, friend, and author in her own right who helped make this book a reality; to my husband, the Rev. Stephen Goldstein, for his support, patience, and love even when I was cranky; to my friends whose feedback on the manuscript was invaluable; to my good friend Tita Buxton for reading the manuscript and sharing her wisdom; to my daughter, Aimee Blair, for keeping me organized and for her encouragement and input; to Nancy and Finlay Schaef, Toni and Skip Lundborg, and the Buxtons for providing quiet, beautiful spaces in which to write.

about the author

Photo © by Julia Luckett.

Pamela Blair, PhD, is a holistic psychotherapist, spiritual counselor, and personal coach with a private practice. She has written for numerous magazines, appeared on radio and television talk shows, and co-authored a bestselling book on grief entitled *I Wasn't Ready to Say Goodbye*. She lives in Shelburne, VT. Visit her online at *www.pamblair.com*.

hampton roads publishing company

. . . for the evolving human spirit

Hampton Roads Publishing Company publishes books on a variety of subjects, including spirituality, health, and other related topics.

For a copy of our latest trade catalog, call (978) 465-0504 or visit our distributor's website at *www.redwheelweiser.com*. You can also sign up for our newsletter and special offers by going to *www.redwheelweiser.com/newsletter*.